50 Ways to Tap the Power of the Sacraments

How you and your family can live grace-filled lives

Bert Ghezzi

Our Sunday Visitor Publishing Division
Our Sunday Visitor, Inc.
Huntington, Indiana 46750

ISBN: 0-87973-747-6
LCCCN: 94-68929

PRINTED IN THE UNITED STATES OF AMERICA
Cover design by Rebecca J. Heaston
747

For John, Paul, Elaine & Vince, Stephen,
Peter, Clare, and Mary

Contents

Acknowledgments

Thirty years ago when I first read Clifford Howell, S.J.'s *Of Sacraments and Sacrifice*, I felt like I had discovered gold — it was a eureka experience. It seemed as though Howell was strolling through my mind and throwing switches that caused dormant concepts to spring to life. Truths I had memorized from the *Baltimore Catechism* that had always seemed as flat and lifeless as cardboard cutouts assumed flesh, breath, and life.

Reading Howell's life-changing classic again inspired me to write *50 Ways to Tap the Power of the Sacraments*, and his practical sacramental theology undergirds many of its articles. Maybe some of Howell's grace will rub off on it and you'll find a gold nugget or two here.

I can't tell you where you may find a copy of *Of Sacraments and Sacrifice* (Collegeville, IN: The Liturgical Press, 1952) because, sad to say, it's out of print. Try a book search company or the interlibrary loan service. But please don't ask to borrow my copy. I'd hate to have to say no to a reader!

Introduction

*"Put Christ first, because he put us first,
and let nothing deter us from loving him."*

St. Cyprian of Carthage

What Do the Sacraments Have to Do With Life?

"Do you know what happened to Mary today?" I asked my family. "Today she received the Holy Spirit and became God's own child. That's the most important thing that happened in the world today, but you won't see it in the newspaper or on the six o'clock news."

We had just returned home from the baptism of Mary, our seventh child, and I had decided to seize the opportunity to speak to my family about the extraordinary realities of the Christian life. The family was assembled in the living room, all dressed up and squirming uncomfortably. I held Mary up as a sign of the realities I was proclaiming, making the baby herself a tiny, wiggly sacrament. I wanted to make a dramatic statement that would grab them and drive home truths they had heard many times before. I wanted to hear my kids say, "Aha! So that's what it's all about."

"Do you realize," I asked, "that all of American history, all the cities we build, all the music, art, buildings, laws, governments — everything — are like a squashed bug compared to Mary? All the things we make will someday cease to exist. They will be destroyed or fade away, but Mary will live forever.

"When Mary dies," I continued, "she will live with God forever."

At this point my son Peter, then nine years old, began to wave his hand with a question, and I thought that I may have gotten through to him.

"Dad," he asked, "can we pray now for my soccer game?"

Well, I thought, the truth will catch up with him and the others later, as it did with me.

I've had my own "Ahas!" — especially at the baptisms of my seven children. Each time I was awestruck by the mystery that this tiny human was now living God's own life. Participating in the rituals startled me with the truth I had once learned by rote: God had humbled himself to share in our humanity so that we could share in his divinity.

Even so I still have a hard time fathoming that my own humanity shares in Christ's divinity. Amid the daily routines of family life, my humanity prevails. As a husband and father I don't usually *feel* very divine, and as I see it, my life does not *look* very divine. Perhaps you feel the same.

Every day is filled with the same mundane activities, which sometimes I regard as chances to serve and sometimes as miserable drudgeries. In the evening, after fighting traffic, helping pull dinner together, watching little girls play softball, and paying bills, I flop on the couch and wonder: Is *this* really my share of divine life? Yes, of course it is, but I'm not seeing it right.

The Sacraments Bring Good Things to Life. I am like the disciples who walked with Jesus along the Emmaus road. He is with me, but I don't always recognize him. "On that day," he promised, "you will realize that I am in my Father and you are in me and I in you" (John 14:20). Well, I don't realize it often enough. I trudge along with my blinders on, missing the best part of reality. Perhaps you do, too. Haven't I seen you on the same road?

Jesus' companions on the Emmaus road did not recognize him until he broke bread with them. It's the same with us. In the celebration of the sacraments, especially the Eucharist, we have the opportunity to meet Jesus and acknowledge that we are living in him. Every day, every moment, without feeling much like it, without always seeing it, we are living in Christ.

The Lord gave us the Eucharist and the other sacraments as reminders of the life we live in him. They are actions we do "in remembrance of him." But the sacraments are not empty memories of bygone events. They are sources of Christlife that carry all the power of his ministry and death to us in the present. Their simple, dramatic signs not only make us aware of our divine lives, they vivify us with divine energy. They use things we can feel, see, taste, smell, and hear, like pouring water, breaking bread, drinking wine, touching with oil, and speaking words to unite us mysteriously to Jesus. They bring him to us smack in the middle of our daily routines.

Each of the seven sacraments plays an important life-giving role that empowers us for ordinary living.

Baptism, confirmation, and the Eucharist are sacraments of initiation because they establish and maintain our union with the Lord.

- Baptism cleanses us spiritually and plunges us into God's life, creating a Father-child relationship that will last forever.
- In confirmation, the Holy Spirit comes to us with gifts and graces — practical tools that assist us on our journey.

- The Lord nourishes us with life-giving food, his own body and blood in the Eucharist.

Two social sacraments increase life in Christ.

- Matrimony provides continuous spiritual support for marriage relationships and family living and involves couples with God in creating new human lives.
- In holy orders the Holy Spirit empowers priests with a share in Christ's mediation, enabling them to perform the sacramental actions that give and sustain our divine lives.

Two sacraments ensure our spiritual and physical health.

- Sinful and broken, we meet Jesus in the sacrament of reconciliation. There the Lord, who died for our sins, forgives us personally, as he did the woman caught in adultery (John 8:3-11), and heals us, as he did the man born blind (John 9:1-41).
- The touch of the Spirit in the anointing of the sick brings physical and spiritual healing to us, restoring our health and preparing those near death for direct and personal union with God.

The sacraments are like power plants that generate a vast supply of supernatural energy. They make God's power available to us, and we can use as much or as little as we choose. They do their life-giving and life-sustaining work whether we're aware of it or not.

But when we approach the sacraments with little appreciation, understanding, or faith, we draw much less spiritual power from them than they provide. Then we are like people who sit shivering in dark houses, not realizing that by flipping a few switches, we could turn on the heat and the lights. The slogan of a great electric appliance company could be a banner headline on an advertisement for the sacraments: We bring good things to life! But to make that come true we must actively tap their power.

Removing Obstacles to Grace. Sometimes our experience with sacraments has become an obstacle that prevents our participating in them. Many Catholics, for example, stay away from the sacrament of reconciliation because once, long ago, they had bad experiences with confession. Many of us, too, live a spiritual half-life, failing to tap the power of the Holy Spirit we receive in confirmation because we do not view the sacrament accurately. We approach it as the end of the journey instead of as a new beginning, the destination instead of an important milestone along the way.

For many the biggest obstacle to fully applying the supernatural power of the sacraments is plain old passivity. We may go through the motions at Mass, for example, unaware that we are offering ourselves as gifts to God in a perfect act of worship. Or we may receive communion unmoved by the significant reality that in it God accepts us and enfolds us in an intimate union with himself. Perhaps the most underutilized sacrament of all is matrimony. Wives and husbands, fathers and mothers don't rely enough on its ample graces to face the daily grind of marriage and family life.

We can revitalize our Christian lives by taking some steps that will sweep away such blocks to grace and let the sacraments channel God's power to us. To draw maximum benefit from the sacraments — to release divine energy that obstacles may have dammed up for years — we must expand our understanding of certain Christian truths and make some decisions to apply them. Our becoming fully Christ-empowered is a matter of thinking and doing. We must think about the difference Christian realities make and do things differently to apply them to our lives.

Grasping the implications of three key truths and acting on them can help us draw maximum benefit from the sacraments, making us fully empowered in Christ. They are:

- Supernatural life. The Lord allows us to share in his own divine life.
- The body of Christ. The Lord has incorporated us into the Church, a living organism of which Christ is the head and we are the members.
- The sacramental principle. The Lord has arranged that the sacraments supernaturally accomplish in us what they signify.

Jesus himself spoke about these realities, and was concerned that we understand them and conform to them. The night before he died, he spoke extensively about them, ensuring that his disciples, who occasionally appeared to be spiritually blind, would at last see what he was all about. As a cure to my own recurring spiritual blindness, I like to read these last words of Jesus. You might also find it helpful. (See John, chapters 13 to 17.)

Supernatural Life. As Christians we live a supernatural life, a life above what's humanly possible, because the Father has given us a share of his own divine life. In our baptisms, God fulfilled Jesus' promises that the Father would send the Holy Spirit to be with us forever (John 14:16) and that he and the Father would come to us and make their home with us (John 14:23). Living the supernatural life means that we are members of God's intimate family.

Jesus chose the image of a vine to illustrate this teaching about life in the Spirit. (See John 15:1-10.) "Abide in me, and I in you," he said. "I am the vine, you are the branches. He who abides in me, and I in him, he it is that bears much fruit, for apart from me you can do nothing" (John 15:4, 5-6). Every part of a grape vine lives the same "grape" life because the same life principle animates every root, branch, and grape. Likewise every baptized Christian lives a divine life because the Holy Spirit himself animates every one of God's children.

This truth has profound practical implications. Sharing divine life enables us to do some things appropriate only to God. At Mass, for example, we can offer perfect worship, something no human being could ever do apart from Christ. Because the Holy Spirit is in us, we can also do the most ordinary things in the most extraordinary way. We can read a book, mow a lawn, cook a meal, change a diaper — all in the Spirit. We can do everything with Jesus because he said apart from him we can do nothing.

The Body of Christ. God could have bestowed supernatural life on us individually in direct, personal gifts. But instead he chose to give us divine life by incorporating us into the Church, an organism that is already living it. Scripture speaks of the Church as the body of Christ, an image that depicts the way God transmits supernatural life to his children. (See 1 Corinthians 12:12-31.) Just as every human cell gets its life from participation in the body, so every Christian receives life from participation in the body of Christ.

Jesus himself again used the image of a vine to explain this truth. Every root and branch, every stem and tendril, every leaf and grape — all get their life only because they are part of the vine. Apart from it they have no life at all. The same is true for us. "As the branch cannot bear fruit by itself," he said, "unless it abides in the vine, neither can you, unless you abide in me" (John 15:4).

The Sacramental Principle. When Jesus was on earth, he accomplished his ministry through his physical body. With his voice he proclaimed the good news of the kingdom and with his hands he fed the hungry and healed the sick. Now he works through us in the Church. We have the privilege of continuing his service to humankind. Thus Christ's actions become our actions, and some of these are sacraments. For example, the conferral of new life in baptism is an action of the body of Christ. That's why this sacrament is appropriately celebrated during Mass when the community is assembled for worship.

The sacraments, especially baptism, confirmation, and the Eucharist, channel God's life to us. They are signs and, like other signs that we use, they communicate to us through our senses. But the Lord works through the sacraments in an extraordinary way that makes them different from every other sign. He has arranged that the sacraments supernaturally accomplish in us what they naturally signify. This is called the sacramental principle.

Other familiar signs cannot cause anything. A traffic sign can tell us to stop or not to turn left. But traffic signs cannot make us stop or prevent us from turning. However, the Lord works through the sacraments, making the realities they designate happen. In baptism, for example, a person is immersed in water as a sign that he or she has been buried in Christ's death in order to rise to a new, supernatural life. We do not *pretend* that the candidate shares in the Lord's death and resurrection. The death and resurrection of Christ really become the death and resurrection of the person baptized.

Take the Eucharist as another example. The Mass is not a dramatic reenactment of the Last Supper or of Calvary. Jesus established the Eucharist as a *re-presentation* of his sacrifice. In the sacrament the bread and wine become the body and blood of the Lord. They are signs that make present what they signify — the cross, the empty tomb, and all their saving power. When the hymn asks, "Were you there when they crucified my Lord?" we can answer, "Why, yes, I *am* there each time I celebrate the sacrament of the Eucharist."

What We Must Do. Christian teaching about the supernatural life, the body of Christ, and the sacramental principle give us a new vision of our Christian lives and the important role the sacraments play. The sacraments are doors to the sacred, openings that lead us into the

Lord's presence. They serve us by creating opportunities for us to meet Jesus. But knowing these truths alone is not enough to help us become Christ-empowered. Our emphasis must not be on the sacraments, but on the life they initiate and sustain in us.

When we meet the Lord in the sacraments, he empowers us to live our human lives divinely. He brings the transforming power of the cross to bear in our ordinary routines. He releases healing graces that prepare us to trade bad behaviors for good. He turns us to our neighbors equipping us for loving service. But we must act in response to his promptings. We need to put grace into action.

What we can do to tap the power the Lord gives us in the sacraments is the subject of this book. In the fifty chapters that follow, you will find hundreds of suggested responses and actions. But all the ways of applying divine energy described here can be summed up under these four headings: know, grow, show and tell, and do. To be Christ-empowered we must *know* the Christian life, *grow* in it, *show and tell* the Christian way to others, and *do* what it requires.

- Know. Understanding the Christian life and the sacraments increases our awareness of what the Lord wants to do for us and disposes us to receive it.
- Grow. Developing our personal relationship with the Lord enables us to draw maximum strength from the sacraments and use it wisely.
- Show and tell. Setting an example of empowered Christian living and telling others about its source in Christ and the sacraments deepens our union with God and the Church.
- Do. Taking an active approach to applying sacramental graces enables the Holy Spirit to move us ahead on our Christian journey.

Help for Parents. While anyone can benefit from these fifty chapters, parents will find them especially helpful for their big job of introducing the Christ-empowered life to their families. The articles devote more attention to parents than they do to children. That's because parental example is critical to effectively introducing children to Christian living.

No matter how different children think they are, they will tend to become like their parents. As they grow up and dig down for resources for living, they will come up with their parents' spiritual heritage. Since we don't want to leave our kids spiritually impoverished, we must give them a robust example of Christ-empowered living for them to imitate now and to fall back on later.

Parents will find it somewhat easier to involve younger children in tapping the power of the sacraments. The stories and the rituals of the sacraments appeal to their innate appreciation of drama and mystery. But as they get older, children get bored easily, and the sacraments may appear to them to be empty shows. How can we, for example, interest teenagers in the liturgy of the Eucharist? We can't, unless they are coming to know the one whom we worship at Mass.

Parents who want to see their teens become Christ-empowered must specialize in show and tell. In addition to presenting a good example of Christian living, we must tell our kids about our own relationship with God. Our witness will demonstrate to them that God is a real person who loves them, cares for them, and wants them to know and love him. Until teens begin to know God and relate to him, they won't get much out of the sacraments because, more than anything, the sacraments are opportunities for meeting Jesus. If our kids don't know him, they will not recognize him in the sacraments.

Maybe my son Peter's prayer request was not off the mark as a response to my little speech at Mary's baptism. After all, the Christ-empowered life and the sacraments that fuel it have everything to do with life, including a nine-year-old's soccer game.

How to Use This Book

50 Ways to Tap the Power of the Sacraments is designed to be practical, so each article contains elements that help you think about the topic and do something about it. Each unit concludes with questions for discussion and reflection, personal and family application ideas, and suggested resources.

Individually, you can read it through or just dip in anywhere you like. Groups may study the units from one to fifty, or they may limit their attention to a segment such as "Empowering Your Family" or "Empowered for Personal Growth."

The appendix contains a pattern for use at group meetings especially designed for Catholic parents.

The Sacraments — Empowering Us in Christ

> **"** *Good behavior does not always lead to good worship; whereas good worship must always lead to good behavior.* **"**
>
> Clifford Howell, S.J.

1 Why Christian Life Is *Super*

 The sacraments give us a supernatural life that enables us to participate in activities that only God can do.

Blessed be the God and Father of our Lord Jesus Christ, who has blessed us in Christ with every spiritual blessing in the heavenly places. Ephesians 1:3

Corky, our family dog, is a wonderful pet. He is friendly, affectionate, obedient, and playful. He is the first one to greet me when I come home. Sometimes I imagine that one day he might welcome me by saying, "Hi, Bert. Boy am I glad you're home! Let's go for a walk, or maybe you'd rather just relax and talk about world affairs." Now that would be an event!

If Corky could converse with me, he would be doing something above his nature. He would be living a *super*natural life because he would be taking part in an activity appropriate only to human beings.

Similarly, living in Christ enlarges our human powers. By begetting us as sons and daughters, the Father has given us a share in divine life. Consequently, we can do some things that are above our human natures. We live a supernatural life that allows us to participate in activities appropriate only to God.

The terms "supernatural life" and "sharing divine life" are theological and may conceal from us the reality of what the Lord has done. The plain truth is that God himself has come to live in us. He has given us his Holy Spirit, making us his close friends. Sharing divine life means having intimacy with God.

Because of our relationship with the Lord, we mere human beings now have these divine possibilities, all of them supernatural, available only because God has enlarged our human natures:

- We have direct access to God. The children of God can confidently approach the heavenly throne to speak with their Father.
- We can worship God with a perfect sacrifice. All previous human efforts to appease God with sacrifices were inadequate.

But at Mass, united to Christ and led by his representative, we offer ourselves to the Father in the perfect sacrifice of the cross.

- We can do things that Jesus did, extending his ministry to our world. We can use our gifts to serve others and draw them to the Lord. We can participate in the sacramental actions through which Christ gives new life.
- We have the gift of faith, the superhuman ability to believe what God has revealed and to trust him for everything. Faith enables us to expect the Lord to intervene in our lives — directly, sacramentally, really.
- We have the supernatural ability to love unconditionally. Love empowers us to serve others in ways that attract them to Christ.
- We acquire a family resemblance to God. The sons and daughters of God become like him through the activity of the Holy Spirit. He produces in us the fruit of the Spirit, dispositions that enable us to act as Jesus did.
- We have the gift of hope — an inspired confidence that God's will and ways will ultimately prevail. With a hopeful perspective, we can approach our lives with anticipation, expecting the Lord to bring good out of the evil we encounter in the world.
- We have the supernatural capacity to see God face to face when we pass through death to our heavenly reward.

All of these magnifications come to us through the sacraments, and as we shall see, they all help us to tap the power of the sacraments more effectively and apply it in daily life.

❧

Thank you, Lord Jesus Christ,
For all the benefits and blessings
which you have given me,
For all the pains and insults
which you have borne for me.
Merciful Friend, Brother and Redeemer,
May I know you more clearly,
Love you more dearly,
And follow you more nearly,
Day by day.

St. Richard of Chichester

For Discussion

- In what sense do Christians live a supernatural life?
- In what ways does intimacy with God enlarge our human natures?

For Reflection

- At what times in my life have I been most aware of my intimacy with God?
- What can we do to help all family members appreciate and appropriate the benefits of supernatural life? What could we do in the next few months? What can we do over the next few years?

Application Ideas

- This week have a brief family conversation about supernatural life. Use the idea of a pet that can talk to illustrate the point.
- Individually or in your family group, study the prayer of St. Richard of Chichester. Ask these questions:
    - What are some of the benefits and blessings the Lord has given us?
    - Why does the prayer call Jesus our Friend? Our Brother? Our Redeemer?
- St. Richard's prayer asks Christ for greater knowledge, love, and obedience. Use it in your personal prayer this week. Make copies for everyone and use it as part of your family prayer time.

Resources

Catechism of the Catholic Church, nos. 1996 to 2005.
Edward D. O'Connor, C.S.C., *The Catholic Vision* (Our Sunday Visitor: 1-800-348-2440), 338-342.

2 Living in Christ

🐛 *We get new life in Christ — a life that means real intimacy with God — from our participation in a Christian community.*

"If a man loves me, he will keep my word, and my Father will love him, and we will come to him and make our home with him." John 14:23

When I was a sophomore in college, I became friends with a group of students and teachers who were dedicated to Christ and to the renewal of his Church. Associating with these young Catholics was an eye-opening experience for me. They taught me what it means to live in Christ.

They invited me to join them for morning prayer before class which I did nearly every day that year. We used a layperson's version of the breviary, the forerunner to *The Liturgy of the Hours*, the Church's official prayer book of psalms, hymns, and readings. This group of friends introduced me to the idea of actively participating in the liturgy, which was a novelty at a time when the celebrant recited the Mass in Latin. But what struck me most about my friends was their familiarity with Christ. They spoke with excitement about loving the Lord and serving his people.

About midway through the year, the group decided to have a weekly Scripture study, another novelty for Catholics who thought studying the Bible was something only Protestants did. Our reading and discussion of the gospel of John on Wednesday afternoons was my first exposure to serious study of Scripture. It also occasioned a spiritual awakening for me.

During that Bible study, truths that I had learned as a child exploded with meaning for me. Verses like these caught my attention: "In that day you will know that I am in my Father, and you in me, and I in you. . . . If a man loves me, he will keep my word, and my Father will love him, and we will come to him and make our home with him"

(John 14:20, 23). I had always believed in the doctrine of the Trinity, but I discovered then that I had a share in the Trinity's life.

From childhood I had believed in eternal life, but reading John expanded my limited notions about it: "And this is eternal life, that they know thee the only true God, and Jesus Christ whom thou hast sent" (John 17:3). The thought that I could intimately know God changed my life. The Lord's presence made ordinary things extraordinary. My work, study, meals, friendships, play, worship, rest — all took on a new dimension. Everything became more satisfying because of the Lord's touch.

John also taught me that Christ was *in me* because God had put me *in Christ*. "I am the vine, you are the branches," Jesus said. "He who abides in me, and I in him, he it is that bears much fruit, for apart from me you can do nothing" (John 15:5). Like a branch that receives its life from the vine, we receive our Christlife from an organism that already lives it, the Church. The Lord put the sacraments in the Church to bring us to life in Christ. Baptism, the Eucharist, and the other sacraments are the sources from which his divine life flows to us.

For me, that group of college friends thirty years ago — Bill, Josey, Tom, Dorothy, Jack, Lorraine, Don, and a few others — was the vine where I discovered my life in Christ and began to live it more fully.

❧

St. Patrick's Breastplate
**Christ, be with me, Christ before me, Christ behind me,
Christ in me, Christ beneath me, Christ above me,
Christ on my right, Christ on my left,
Christ where I lie, Christ where I sit, Christ where I arise,
Christ in the heart of every one who thinks of me,
Christ in the mouth of every one who speaks of me,
Christ in every eye that sees me,
Christ in every ear that hears me.
Salvation is of the Lord.
Salvation is of the Lord,
Salvation is of the Christ.
May your salvation Lord, be ever with us.**

For Discussion
- What do the terms "eternal life" and "living in Christ" mean?
- How does God give us a share in his life?
- What can we do to live more fully in Christ?

For Reflection
- How has living in Christ affected my daily activities? What one thing could I do to become more aware of my life in Christ?
- How aware are family members of their lives in Christ? What could we do to increase our awareness?

Application Ideas
- For the next week, pray St. Patrick's Breastplate in your prayer time and/or with the family. Make copies for everyone. Use the prayer time as an occasion to talk personally about living in Christ.
- Have the family read and talk about John, chapter 15, verses 1 to 10. (See the Introduction, p. 17.) Use a real vine or any plant to illustrate these main points:
    - The vine or plant is a living picture of the Church. The vine represents Jesus and, by extension, the Church, the body of Christ. We are the branches, leaves, tendrils, flowers, and so on that make up the Church.
    - Just as the plant has a source that gives life to every part of the plant, so the Holy Spirit is the source of life for everyone in the Church. Every part of a grapevine lives "grape" life and every person of the Church lives the life of Christ.
    - Just as a leaf or stem gets its life from the plant, so we too get our Christlife from the Church, mainly from the sacraments.

Resources
Catechism of the Catholic Church, nos. 31-35.
Edward D. O'Connor, C.S.C., *The Catholic Vision* (Our Sunday Visitor: 1-800-348-2440), 348-356.

3 Christian Body Language

The service Jesus once performed in his physical body, he now continues through us in his mystical body, the Church.

Now you are the body of Christ and individually members of it. 1 Corinthians 12:27

"But why do we have to go to Mass?" asks your child.

Think twice before you give an answer like, "Because we're Catholics and Catholics have to go to Mass on Sunday."

Sometimes we speak about the Church as though it were just another organization. We approach it as a religious club with membership requirements, presiding officers, required meetings, and dues. This limited view helps explain why many young people don't connect with the Church. In their experience, organizations are not life-giving, so they choose not to bother with what they perceive to be another lifeless structure.

The Church is not a lifeless organization but a life-giving organism. Scripture says it is the body of Christ. Christ is the head of his body and we are his members. This powerful biblical analogy teaches us how to live as Christians and how to apply the spiritual energy of the sacraments.

Thinking about our physical bodies helps us grasp the significance of the body of Christ. We are composed of many parts — cells, blood, bones, skin, eyes, mouths, hands, feet and so on — but our life unites them into a single organism. It's the same with Christ and us. Millions of believers form one body in Christ because the same source of vital energy binds us together and gives us life. That life-giving source is the Holy Spirit and that life that unites us is God's own.

As human beings, we use our bodies to express ourselves and to have an effect on the persons and things around us. Through our bodies we communicate, express affection, work, serve, celebrate, and relate in many other ways.

Jesus was once a human being who used his body to work among us. He proclaimed good news. He touched the sick to heal them. He taught us how to live. He cared for the poor. He caressed little children. He served others, even cooking breakfast for his weary friends (John 21:9-12). He worshiped his Father. Ultimately he used his body to offer himself on the cross as the sacrifice that saved us and restored our union with God.

After his ascension, Christ still needed a body to continue his ministry on the earth. He needed human beings to reach out to other human beings. So he chose to create a new body, the Church, with him as head and us as members.

As I live in all the parts of my body and act through them, Christ lives in all the parts of his body and acts through them. We are the eyes of Christ who see others suffering and the feet of Christ that rush to their aid. We are Christ's mouth announcing good news of salvation, teaching our kids how to live as Christians, and giving advice to the confused. We are the hands of Christ that feed the hungry, build houses for the homeless, heal the sick, and offer praise to the Father.

Christ's actions have become our actions, and our actions his. This is especially true of the sacraments. Christ brings salvation and new life to human beings through baptism, confirmation, the Eucharist, reconciliation, matrimony, holy orders, and anointing of the sick. As members of his body, we also do these sacred things with him.

❦

We are united with Christ, who is God, with a closeness which no human relationship even comes near. Mother and son are close, but they are still two. Our union with Christ is closer than that union, at its very closest, could ever be. Every Catholic is closer to us by the union he or she and we have with Christ than is any member of our family by natural kinship. If we began to treat one another accordingly, it would be a new world.

Frank Sheed

For Discussion
• In what ways is the body of Christ like the human body?
• How could applying this teaching change our social environments?

For Reflection

- In what ways do I serve in the body of Christ? How can I make myself more available to Christ for his work?
- Do all family members understand that the Church is the body of Christ? What one thing could we do differently to live this teaching more fully?

Application Ideas

- This week invite each person to do one act of service for someone outside the family, something they would not have to do as part of their ordinary routines. Each evening at dinner have one person describe what he or she did and tell how it was also Christ's action.
- Individually or as a group, study 1 Corinthians, chapter 12, verses 12 to 31. Ask these questions:
  - What is the role of the Holy Spirit in the body of Christ?
  - Why did God create a diversity of gifts among members of the body?

Resources

Catechism of the Catholic Church, nos. 787-795; 1267.
Edward D. O'Connor, C.S.C., *The Catholic Vision* (Our Sunday Visitor: 1-800-348-2440), 374-377.

4 The Most Extraordinary Event

> *The sacraments make the reality and power of Christ's death and resurrection present for us now.*

"Do this in remembrance of me." 1 Corinthians 11:24

Some historians say that D-Day, June 6, 1944, may have been the most important day in the twentieth century. On that day 170,000 American troops landed on the beaches of Normandy in a surprise attack against Hitler's armies. It was the greatest battle in American history. At the cost of thousands of lives, these courageous young soldiers launched the campaign that would finally liberate Europe from the murderous Nazi conquest and put an end to the Holocaust.

I was born in 1941 a few weeks before Pearl Harbor, and I turned three years old a few weeks after D-Day. I was too young to be aware of these historic events, but my earliest childhood memories are vaguely associated with World War II. I was raised in Pittsburgh, Pennsylvania, a city that feared Nazi air attacks because its steel mills were helping turn the tide. I remember watching my parents cover windows for blackouts and huddling with them under the kitchen table during air-raid drills.

As an adult I have more memories of the war because I read books like Winston Churchill's *The Second World War* and William Stevenson's *A Man Called Intrepid.* For seven years as a college history teacher, I even lectured about it.

The celebration of the fiftieth anniversary of D-Day also helped me remember that event. Films, documentaries, articles, speeches, interviews with veterans, news reports from Normandy's cemeteries were fitting remembrances. They made the event "come alive" for me. It was almost like being there.

Of course, like all events in history, I cannot be present at D-Day and D-Day cannot be really present to me. The only way that D-Day or any historical event can be present to us is as ideas — representations in our minds that we get from books, pictures, films, monuments, or eye-witness stories. The event itself cannot be present to us because the passage of time has locked it in the past beyond our reach. Time machines exist only in fictions like "Back to the Future."

Only one historic event is not subject to this limit, and it is the most important of all. The death and resurrection of Jesus Christ nearly two thousand years ago is the central event of human history. With his body viciously stretched out on the cross and his blood drained out, Jesus at the moment of his greatest weakness won the cosmic war between God and the forces of Satan, sin, and death. Like all historical events, the work of Christ would have remained locked in the past had God not done something special. The Lord wanted to make Christ's death and resurrection present for human beings in all ages. But there was no way in the natural order that it could be done.

God had to create a new reality that would make it possible for the death and resurrection of Jesus to be present to us. So he established the sacraments to bring the work of Christ to us now.

We were not standing at the cross or in the garden, but the sacraments mysteriously take us to Calvary and to the empty tomb. We stand as close to Jesus as did his mother and the beloved disciple (John 19:25-27), and we encounter him as Mary did on the first Easter (John 20:11-18).

The sacraments do not repeat the historical event. Christ died once for all. But they bring us into the presence of the cross and risen Christ sacramentally, so that all the power, graces, and benefits of that greatest event of the past flow to us now. We call this reality the sacramental principle.

❦

When we eat this bread and drink this cup we proclaim your death, Lord Jesus, until you come in glory.

Memorial Acclamation,
Liturgy of the Eucharist

For Discussion

• How is Jesus' death like all other historical events?
• How do the sacraments make the Lord's death and resurrection different from all other historical events?

For Reflection

- On what occasions in my life have I been most aware of Christ's presence in the sacraments?
- To what extent does my family approach the sacraments as opportunities to come into Christ's presence?
- How can we help each other increase our experience of the Lord's presence in the sacraments?

Application Ideas

- Conduct a discussion about favorite past events.
    - Ask everyone to think about an event in the past.
    - Each person should choose either a favorite personal memory (going fishing with Grandma) or a historical event that interests them (the Declaration of Independence).
    - Invite everyone to describe the event and why it's important to them.
    - When all have shared, ask the group how these events could be present to us now.
    - Ask the group if it is aware of any past event that can be experienced in the present.
    - Lead the group to the conclusion that the death and resurrection of Christ is present to us through the sacraments.
    - Talk about one of the acclamations we proclaim after the consecration at Mass. We should be alert when we say these words because the sacrament takes us to be near Christ at Calvary.

Resources

Catechism of the Catholic Church, nos. 1115; 1118.
Edward D. O'Connor, C.S.C., *The Catholic Vision* (Our Sunday Visitor: 1-800-348-2440), 388-391.

5 Signs That Do What They Say

❧ *Sacraments are signs that accomplish in our spirits what they signify in our senses.*

He put his fingers into his ears, and he spat and touched his tongue; and looking up to heaven, he sighed, and said to him, "*Ephphatha!*" that is, "Be opened!" And his ears were opened, his tongue was released, and he spoke plainly. Mark 7:33-35

I had not noticed how dependent we are on signs until I found myself in a place that had none.

A week after Hurricane Andrew struck, I drove a van load of ice and water to friends in south Florida. People were demonstrating remarkable resilience, cleaning up and working to restore essentials. But they had not yet begun to replace directional signs, all of which the storm had swept away. Traffic was in great confusion because signal lights were out everywhere and stop signs were gone. I had a difficult time finding my friend's house because there were no longer any street signs.

Signs play a big role in our lives. They inform us about things we want to know. The sign on the bank kiosk says that it's 12 noon and 85 degrees. The golden arches declare that food is right around the corner. Signs make announcements: "This office will be closed Monday." They warn us: "The surgeon general has determined that smoking is dangerous to your health." They give directions: "No right turn." We rely on signs to keep things going smoothly.

Signs are also an important part of our Christian lives. For example, Jesus used dramatic signs to help us understand his actions when he blessed or healed people. He touched lepers and commanded them to "Be clean" (Luke 5:13). He healed a blind man by making clay with saliva and smearing it on his eyes (John 9:6-7). He also established the sacraments as effective signs that accomplish what they signify. Because the sacraments make happen what they declare, they are different from every other sign.

Important as they are, we don't usually expect signs to do anything more than tell us things. Ordinary signs cannot cause what they signify. The bank clock merely announces the time, but cannot affect it. A speedometer shows how fast we are going, but cannot cause us to go at that speed. Even the most persuasive signs cannot make happen what they signify. A television commercial for a perfectly grilled filet mignon may make our mouth water, but it cannot produce the steak.

However, the Lord created the sacraments as signs through which he accomplishes in the supernatural order what these signs signify in the natural order:

- In baptism by God's power, a natural sign of cleansing produces supernatural cleanness.
- A meal of bread and wine provides supernatural nourishment in the Eucharist.
- In confirmation, anointing with chrism and laying on of hands causes supernatural strengthening.
- Confession of sins and the words of absolution restore our supernatural union with God in the sacrament of reconciliation.
- Application of oil causes spiritual healing in the anointing of the sick.
- In matrimony, the public exchange of vows by husband and wife forges a supernatural union in Christ.
- Anointing with oil and laying on of hands in holy orders supernaturally seals a man to serve as a priest.

The Lord uses signs that affect our bodies in order to accomplish what he desires in our spirits. He can produce spiritual effects in us directly, and often does. But he normally chooses to use signs because they suit our human nature. We are spirits encased in bodies. To bring life to our spirits, God touches our bodies.

❧

A sacrament is not only a commemorative sign of something which is now past — the passion of Christ; it is also a demonstrative sign of something now present and caused in us by the passion of Christ — grace; further it is a . . . prophetic sign of something as yet in the future — glory.

St. Thomas Aquinas

For Discussion

• What role do signs play in the Christian life?
• Why did God choose to use signs?

For Reflection

• How well am I using the signs the Lord has established to help me spiritually? What steps could I take to draw more benefit from the sacraments?
• What sacraments have family members experienced personally? To what extent are family members aware that sacraments are signs?

Application Ideas

• Conduct a fifteen-minute family discussion on signs. Ask everyone to choose any sign they like and either bring it or a picture of it to the discussion.
  - Ask each one to explain what his or her sign says.
  - When all have shared, ask everyone if their sign can make what they say happen.
  - Conclude by explaining that sacraments are signs, but they are unlike all other signs because they do in our spirits what they say to our senses.
• Consider continuing the above discussion by displaying several sacramental signs, that is water, bread, wine, and oil. Ask family members to say what they think each item naturally signifies. Then ask the harder questions: What do these natural signs accomplish supernaturally in our souls: Water in baptism? Bread and wine in the Eucharist? Oil in confirmation?

Resources

Catechism of the Catholic Church, nos. 1113-1134.
Edward D. O'Connor, C.S.C., *The Catholic Vision* (Our Sunday Visitor: 1-800-348-2440), 391-393.

6 Praying With Jesus

 *Because we are in Christ, we have a new capacity to pray with him and to have him pray with us.*

Like living stones be yourselves built into a spiritual house, to be a holy priesthood, to offer spiritual sacrifices acceptable to God through Jesus Christ. 1 Peter 2:5

When Jesus was asked to teach us how to pray, he gave us the Our Father. But he did more than give us the words of a beautiful prayer. He arranged that we could pray with him. Through the sacraments, he made his prayer our prayer, and our prayer his.

The ability to pray in a new way is one of the enlargements of our natural powers that we enjoy because the Father put us *in Christ*. Without life in Christ our worship would be limited to our natural capacities. We would be able to pray, but only with the force of "one humanpower." But in Christ our prayer is supernaturally transformed. God enlarged our capacity for worship so that we pray with the force of "one Godpower." As human beings living in Christ, we can pray with divine power because Christ prays in us. The sacraments are the means that the Lord uses to magnify our prayer power.

The first letter of Peter explains how we came to be able to pray with Godpower. When baptism incorporated us into the Church, Peter says, we were given a share in Christ's priesthood. So we were empowered to join him in offering worship to the Father, especially in the celebration of the Eucharist.

Peter used the dramatic image of a spiritual house made of living stones to show that we have the power to worship in a superhuman way. Like the body of Christ, the spiritual house is an analogy for the Church. Jesus is the cornerstone, and we as living stones are being built on him into a spiritual house. We become a holy priesthood in the spiritual house so that we can "offer spiritual sacrifices acceptable to God through Jesus Christ." As a result, when we pray through Jesus, his prayer becomes our prayer, and our prayer becomes his.

Peter's spiritual house analogy emphasizes that the Christian life has essentially to do with worship and prayer. The Lord has magnified our prayer power and made worship a foundation for Christian living. So we must make praying with Jesus a priority for our lives and for our families.

Even though we seem to be the busiest people history has known, we still have many chances to worship. The Church provides many formal opportunities:

- The Mass, Sunday and daily, where we sacramentally offer with Jesus his sacrificial worship;
- The celebration of the sacraments;
- *The Liturgy of the Hours*, the official prayer of the Church (also referred to as the Divine Office), which priests and religious pray with Jesus through the day. Lay people are invited to join in this prayer publicly when parishes celebrate vespers. Some lay people pray an abbreviated version privately or in small groups.

We also have many informal opportunities to use our magnified prayer power:

- We can begin and close our day with personal prayer. The Holy Spirit whom we received in baptism enables us to pray with Jesus even when we pray alone.
- We should pray for and with our kids whenever we can. Pronouncing a blessing, asking for protection, thanking the Lord for a good day — prayers like these are means of empowering our family in Christ and applying the grace of the sacraments.
- We can make a prayer time a regular part of our family lives. This is the most practical way to introduce our kids to praying with Jesus. It's the most effective way to tap the power of the sacraments at home. "Where two or three are gathered in my name," Jesus said, "there am I in the midst of them" (Matthew 18:20).

The Lord's Prayer
Our Father, who art in heaven,
hallowed be thy Name;

thy kingdom come;
thy will be done on earth as it is in heaven.
Give us this day our daily bread;
and forgive us our trespasses
as we forgive those who trespass against us;
and lead us not into temptation,
but deliver us from evil. Amen.

Jesus is our prayer, and He is also the answer to all our prayer. He has chosen to be Himself in us the living song of love, praise, adoration, thanksgiving, intercession and reparation to the Father in the name of the whole creation.

Mother Teresa

For Discussion

- Why can it be said that worship is an essential activity for those who live in Christ?
- What difference does living in Christ make in our worship?

For Reflection

- What difference can praying with Jesus make in my personal prayer? In my worship at Mass?
- How can I and my family make better use of our ability to worship in union with Christ?

Application Ideas

- Use these questions to review your personal prayer time:
  - Am I praying with Jesus as fully and as often as I can?
  - What might I do differently?
- Teach your children the Lord's Prayer. Pray it together every day for one or two weeks. Consider making this prayer a regular part of your daily family routine.

Resources

Catechism of the Catholic Church, nos. 1073; 1174-1178; 1196-1197; 1268; 2598-2616.

Thomas Merton, *Praying the Psalms* (The Liturgical Press: 1-800-858-5450).

7 A "Liturgist"? Who, Me?

🐦 *We are liturgists because we have become collaborators with Christ in continuing his ministry of healing and service.*

We have such a high priest, . . . "a minister in the sanctuary and the true tent." Hebrews 8:1-2

"Liturgy" is a collective term for all of the Church's official worship, including the Mass and the sacraments. While we are familiar with the word, we don't seem to have much awareness of its significant root meaning. But thinking about the origins of the word "liturgy" can help us approach the sacraments with more faith and receive more spiritual strength from them. With a little reflection, we may even feel comfortable calling ourselves "liturgists."

The word "liturgy" comes from two Greek words meaning "public" and "work." A Greek citizen performed a liturgy when he did a work at his own expense for the benefit of the public. For example, a person was a "liturgist" if he built a theater and donated it to the local community. Or a person might construct a temple in honor of a local God, providing his city with a place for sacrifices and worship. Today we could call the Arnold Palmer Hospital for Children and Women a "liturgy" and the great golfer who gave it to the people of Orlando, Florida, a "liturgist."

In this original sense, a liturgy required the collaboration of the recipients. By definition a liturgy had to involve its beneficiaries. The community had to attend the theater, worship at the temple, or bring its sick to the hospital.

The letter to the Hebrews calls Jesus a "minister," an English word that translates the Greek word meaning "a person who performs a liturgy." Jesus is a liturgist because he did a work at his own expense for the benefit of all people. His liturgy was offering his life in the sacrifice of the cross, shedding his blood to gain the redemption of all humankind.

Jesus' work also requires the collaboration of its beneficiaries. We

41

receive salvation by putting faith in Christ's death and resurrection. "If you confess with your lips," Paul says, "that Jesus is Lord and believe in your heart that God raised him from the dead, you will be saved" (Romans 10:9).

Jesus died once for all at Calvary, but his liturgy was not over. He arranged that his sacrifice would continue to be available for us in the sacraments. When we gather at the altar to celebrate the liturgy of the Eucharist or at the font to celebrate a baptismal liturgy, the sacrifice of the cross becomes present to us with all of its saving graces.

Christ's liturgy also calls for our continued collaboration. We are invited to receive the benefits of Jesus' liturgy by joining in the performance of the Eucharistic celebration through which he continues to offer himself to the Father on our behalf. Since the Eucharist is the celebration of the whole community, and not of the priest alone, our participation is essential, not optional.

When he was on the earth, the Lord conducted his ministry through his physical body, but now he conducts his work through us — the body of Christ, the Church. At Mass we offer Christ's sacrifice with him and in the sacraments, we work with him to bring new life and healing to others. We are liturgists because the Lord has called on us to be his collaborators in continuing his liturgy.

❧

The Church . . . earnestly desires that Christ's faithful, when present at this mystery of faith, should not be there as strangers or as silent spectators. On the contrary, through a proper appreciation of the rites and prayers they should participate knowingly, devoutly and actively. They should be instructed by God's word and be refreshed at the table of the Lord's body; they should give thanks to God; by offering the Immaculate Victim, not only through the hands of the priest, but also with him, they should learn to offer themselves too. Through Christ the Mediator, they should be drawn day by day into ever closer union with God and with each other, so that finally God may be all in all.

Vatican Council II
Constitution on the Sacred Liturgy

For Discussion

- In its original meaning, what had to be present for a work to be recognized as a liturgy? Why is Jesus' sacrifice a liturgy?
- Why is our participation in the liturgy an essential and not an option?

For Reflection

- In what sense am I a "liturgist"? How can I take a more active part in the liturgy?
- How actively does my family participate in the liturgy of the Eucharist? What could we do to help each other participate more fully in the liturgy?

Application Ideas

- Individually or as a family, study the quotation above from the *Constitution on the Sacred Liturgy*. Use these questions as guides:
    - How does the Church expect us to prepare for active participation in the liturgy?
    - What does active participation involve?
    - How does my involvement in the liturgy affect my relationship to God?
- Involve younger children in some simple activity that benefits the whole family. For example, let them earn money to purchase the ingredients for a treat that they can help to make.
    - Explain the parallel between what they have done for the family and what Christ has done for the human race.
    - Tell them that at Mass we get to help Jesus do the work he came to do by offering ourselves with him to the Father.

Resources

Catechism of the Catholic Church, nos. 1069-1072.
Mark Searle, *Liturgy Made Simple* (The Liturgical Press: 1-800-858-5450), 11-32.

8 Pray-ers Must Be Do-ers

❦ *The kingdom of God becomes present in the sacraments so that we can work with Christ to restore justice in the world.*

But be doers of the word, and not hearers only. James 1:22

Our Christian lives are not divisible into separate compartments. We cannot be good "pray-ers" without doing, or good "do-ers" without praying. We cannot worship the Lord on Sunday and continue to behave unjustly during the week, for worship and justice are inseparably linked. The letter of James exposes the absurdity of the idea that we could have true worship without justice: "If a brother or sister is ill-clad and in lack of daily food, and one of you says to them, 'Go in peace, be warmed and filled,' without giving them the things needed for the body, what does it profit? So faith by itself, if it has no works, is dead" (James 2:15-17). For the Christian, praise and good works are united in the Holy Spirit who prompts and directs us in both worship and action.

Justice for the Christian is not limited to its legal or constitutional senses that merely set limits on wrongdoing or arbitrate claims. Ours is the justice of God, embodied in his kingdom and revealed in Jesus. In his justice, God seeks to release all creatures from corruption and deformation and to restore them to the purposes for which he created them.

Christ has already established the kingdom of God by his death and resurrection. Now through the sacraments, the Lord makes God's kingdom present in us so that we can work with him to bring God's saving justice to the world. In baptism, for example, we die with Christ to a disjointed world that is organized on principles that do not acknowledge God. We rise with him to live according to the Holy Spirit himself, who leads us to seek the restoration of all things.

The new life of baptism cuts through all differences — cultural, racial, national, economic — so that we come to the Eucharist as brothers and sisters in the Lord's family. At the sacrificial meal, we share the body and blood of Christ. By our participation in the liturgy, we learn to share our diverse gifts. This sharing in God's kingdom that we receive and learn in the sacrament must not stop in the pews, for sharing is an instrument we must use to establish God's justice in our societies.

That truth is embodied in the word "Mass," which derives from the Latin form of the dismissal, "*Ite, missa est,*" "Go, you are dismissed." Now the celebrant dismisses us by charging us to "Go in peace to love and serve the Lord."

Thus we are to embody the love of God we receive in the Eucharist, distributing it freely in the human community. The practice of the first Christians is a model for us. Christians that shared God's abundance in the liturgy also shared with each other from the abundance of their wealth. For example, in the Jerusalem community, "There was not a needy person among them, for as many as were possessors of lands or houses sold them, and brought the proceeds . . . and laid it at the apostles' feet; and distribution was made to each as any had need" (Acts 4:34-35).

The Church has instructed us in practical ways of working for God's justice. Especially helpful are two sets of guidelines that are rooted in Scripture and the tradition of the Church. These are the corporal and spiritual works of mercy:

The Corporal Works of Mercy	**The Spiritual Works of Mercy**
Feed the hungry	Counsel the doubtful
Give drink to the thirsty	Instruct the ignorant
Clothe the naked	Admonish the sinner
Visit the imprisoned	Comfort the afflicted
Shelter the homeless	Forgive offenses
Visit the sick	Bear wrongs patiently
Bury the dead	Pray for the living and the dead

We should measure our Christian action against these standards, for caring for the poor and needy is the test of the genuineness of our Christian love (see James 1:27). Spending ourselves to provide the material and spiritual needs of others is also a training ground for the bigger Christian task of transforming social and political institutions.

It is not bread that constitutes the sacramental sign of the Eucharist, nor oil that is the sacramental sign of confirmation or anointing of the sick, but bread that is broken and shared, the cup of wine passed around for all to drink, the oil applied by one person to another. The sacraments are actions of the body, through which we become present to one another and touch one another's lives.

Mark Searle

For Discussion
• Why and how are worship and justice inseparably linked?

For Reflection
• How has my participation in the sacraments influenced my service to others? Do I try to meet the needs of others by sharing with them?

Application Ideas
• Teach the family the corporal and spiritual works of mercy. Be sure the children understand what each guideline means. Have everyone memorize them and recite them at family prayer times.
• Have the family select one of the corporal works of mercy that it would like to practice. Decide on a simple and limited action such as staffing a soup kitchen on a Saturday afternoon, and do it. Review the activity at a family prayer time by having people share what they learned in the experience.

Resources
Catechism of the Catholic Church, nos. 1068; 1072; 1928-1942.
Mary Ann Kuharski, *Parenting With Prayer* (Our Sunday Visitor: 1-800-348-2440), chapters 18 and 19.

Empowering Your Family

" *The family has received from God its mission to be the first and vital cell of society. It will fulfill this mission if it shows itself to be the domestic sanctuary of the Church through the mutual affection of its members and the common prayer they offer to God, if the whole family is caught up in the liturgical worship of the Church, and if it provides active hospitality and promotes justice and other good works for the service of all the brethren in need.* "

Vatican Council II
Decree on the Apostolate of the Laity

9 If We Don't Tell Our Kids, Who Will?

❦ *Parents must help children find a personal relationship with God by telling them about their own experience with him.*

That which we have seen and heard we proclaim also to you, so that you may have fellowship with us; and our fellowship is with the Father and with his Son Jesus Christ. 1 John 1:3

Parents don't find it easy to talk with their children about God. Sometimes we feel lucky to have conversations with a child at all. But talking with kids about topics like life in Christ, prayer, or the sacraments seems more difficult than discussing almost anything else.

When parents try to talk about religion, kids often respond with signals that we can easily interpret as boredom. They fidget, shift from foot to foot, or look out the window. I think, however, that most kids are not really bored with discussing the things of God. Rather, they show signs of discomfort because they sense the seriousness of the subject and don't know how to respond. They may not be ready to discuss things that affect their lives so profoundly. So parents should not let silence or monosyllabic grunts dissuade them from talking to their children about the Lord. Someday our kids will respond, and we will be glad we made the effort.

It may be parents, not kids, however, who have the most difficulty talking about God. Many are reluctant to raise the subject for a variety of reasons. Some feel that their relationship to God is such a personal matter that talking about it even with their children is an invasion of privacy. Others think that they don't know enough about their faith to do a good enough job of handing it on to their kids. Inertia and inexperience prevent still others from speaking up. But if we don't talk to our children about the Lord, we are depriving them of the thing they need most from us.

We may think that setting a good Christian example for our kids is sufficient. But it's not. If we want our children to join us in fellowship with the Father, Son, and Spirit, we must tell them about the Lord we have come to know and love. We must also explain *why* we live the way we do. Otherwise the children may misunderstand our example, seeing it only as our going through the motions. If we don't tell them about his ways, who will? They may discover the meaning of life in the message of music videos or talk-show hosts. Just the thought of Madonna or Geraldo forming our kids should help us overcome our reticence and start us talking.

❦

Parents talk plentifully of their business and social relationships, but in my experience they rarely speak of their divine relationship. How many parents ever tell their children how they came to meet the living God? Unless that happens, religion for the teenager remains something unreal, to be endured a few classes a week and once on Sunday, until he or she gets sprung.

William J. O'Malley, S.J.

For Discussion
• Why is it important for parents to talk to their children about the Christian life?

For Reflection
• What has been my experience of talking to my children about God and his ways?
• What recent experience of the Lord, the Christian life, or the sacraments could I share with my kids?
• Do I speak to my children about the Lord, the Christian life, and the sacraments? Do I speak personally? Do I put things in my own words?
• Do I create formal opportunities for conversations with my children?

Application Ideas
• Here are some tips for talking to kids about life in Christ:
  - Speak openly about your experience of God. Describe how things like a prayer, Scripture text, Mass, or baptism of a neighbor baby affected you personally. Your sharing will present the Lord to them as someone they should get to know.

- Use your own words to tell your kids about the Lord, life in Christ, and the sacraments. Try to be as correct as you can, but don't worry about it. Right now they need your witness more than they need theological exactness which, though important, can come later.
- Watch for opportunities to have conversations about the Lord and his ways right in the course of daily living.
- Create more formal opportunities for discussions. You can review their catechism lessons each week, or supplement their preparation for first communion or confirmation with family discussions. Family prayer times, Bible studies, reading books together, and bedtime blessings are also chances for conversations. Don't pass them up.
- Don't hesitate to talk to children about topics that might seem too difficult for them to grasp. Some truths they don't understand now, they will discover later. Others will remain mysteries for them, as they do for us.
- Trust the Holy Spirit to guide you and to ensure that you will do a good job in talking with your children about the Lord, life in Christ, and the sacraments.

Resources

Catechism of the Catholic Church, nos. 2225-2226.
Catholic Parent (bimonthly magazine; Our Sunday Visitor: 1-800-348-2440).
Bert Ghezzi, *Guiltless Catholic Parenting from A to Y* (Servant Publications: 1-800-458-8505).
How to Talk to Your Children About . . . (Series of nine booklets on the following topics: Confirmation, Prayer, Reconciliation, Being Catholic, Mary, Death and the Afterlife, Eucharist, Mass, Jesus). Available as single copies or in book form entitled *How to Talk to Your Children About Being Catholic* from Our Sunday Visitor: 1-800-348-2440).

10 Starting a Family Prayer Time

🍎 *Having a regular prayer time is a key way for families to tap the power of the sacraments for daily living.*

"I am with you always." Matthew 28:20

Our family recently started a formal prayer time — again. I would need all my fingers and toes to count the number of times we've had to begin praying together again over the past thirty years. If that weren't fairly normal, I'd be worried.

The Lord lives in our families whether we realize it or not. "I am with you always," Jesus promised (Matthew 28:20). But if we don't speak with him and listen to him, we don't acknowledge his presence. Those times when our family is not praying together, I get the uneasy feeling that, even though the Lord is with us in our home, we are ignoring him. Can you picture him standing nearby wanting to talk and my brushing past him without noticing?

Family prayer is one of the best ways to help children discover that God is neither a vague idea nor a distant Being, but rather a Person who loves them. It helps Mom and Dad know him better, too. When we pray together, we begin to experience the Lord dwelling among us. By communicating with him, we acknowledge his presence, giving him opportunities to reveal himself more fully to each family member.

Family prayer helps us engage the Lord's grace for our daily lives. Because Christ's prayer has become ours and our prayer has become his, it is a way for families to tap the power of the sacraments. When we pray together, we learn God is not indifferent to us. We find that he cares even about the little things that hardly seem to deserve the attention of the One who put the stars in their places. When we pray for a lost key and find it, we grow in faith to pray for bigger things, like a loved one who seems to be lost.

Family prayer also gives us other benefits, including opportunities to:
- Tell our children how we came to know and serve God;
- Instruct them in the teachings of Christ and the Church;
- Involve them in praying for the people in the world around them;

- Teach them how to use the sacraments as means for growth in Christ;
- Introduce them to reading and applying Scripture;
- Resolve family problems prayerfully.

But be careful not to expect too much. There are limits to what family prayer can do. It will focus us on the Lord, but it will not magically transform kids into spiritual giants. Nor parents either. Family life is messy on many levels, and praying together will not change that condition much, except to help us put it all in divine perspective. Yes, conflicts will even pop up during prayer times — clandestine pinches, judgmental snickers, squabbles over who gets to read the Bible verse. No reason to get discouraged, but all the more reason to pray.

❦

Make yourself a promise that praying together before bedtime will be a must from now on. Never mind the wiggling tot, testy teen, or endless distractions. . . . Something gentle and good occurs when we take a few moments to pray together as a family. We all come away a bit transformed and tranquil.

Mary Ann Kuharski

For Discussion
- What are the benefits of having a family prayer time?

For Reflection
- In what ways are we praying together as a family? What could we do differently to improve our family prayer?

Application Ideas
- Here are some tips you will find helpful for starting a family prayer time:
  - Couples must agree that they want to have family prayer and how they want it to go. It won't work well if one parent is not involved.
  - Work out a plan before starting or changing family prayer. Determine the why, who, what, when, where, and how for your prayer time.

- Consider your kids' ages and adapt accordingly. Keeping family prayer short and simple suits all age groups.
- Gather up resources in advance — Bibles, song sheets, prayer books, rosaries — whatever you decide to use.
- Choose a time and place that will work well everyday. Try to pick a time when all can be present, especially teenage children with busy schedules.
- Explain to the children what you are going to do and why, before you start up or make a change in your family prayer.
- Set a good example. Both Mom and Dad must pray aloud themselves, showing the children how it's done.
- Involve everyone in some way. Let one child read a Scripture verse, another select a song, another pray for intentions.
- Talk directly to God. For example, use the personal "Lord, I ask you for . . ." not the impersonal "I want to ask the Lord for. . . ."
- Keep starting over. When one approach fails or ceases to be helpful, prayerfully review what you've been doing and alter it in some way.

Resources

Catechism of the Catholic Church, nos. 2685; 2688; 2691; 2698; 2700-2704.

Mary Ann Kuharski, *Parenting With Prayer* (Our Sunday Visitor: 1-800-348-2440).

Bert Ghezzi, *Keeping Your Kids Catholic* (Servant Publications: 1-800-458-8505), chapter 4.

11 Together at Mass

 *Worshiping together at Mass creates a focus that gives a family a life-shaping Catholic orientation.*

And they devoted themselves to the apostles' teaching and fellowship, to the breaking of bread and the prayers. Acts 2:42

Because Sunday is on the weekend, it feels to us like the last day of the week. We see Monday as the day when everything starts up again. But for Christians, Sunday is the first day of the week. It is the day we commemorate that pivotal Sunday when Jesus transformed humankind by rising from the dead.

Early Christians gathered voluntarily for Sunday worship. Today Church law makes it an obligation for Catholics. But if we regard it only as a duty, we miss the point, and so will our kids. Rather, we must approach Mass for what it really is — an opportunity for us to meet Jesus and to join him in his worship of the Father. There's no better way for human beings to begin their week.

At Sunday Mass we assemble with others as a family "cell" in the local body of Christ. We gather to honor God and to replenish our spiritual energy for the coming week. We hear the Lord's voice in the proclamation of his word. We exercise our supernatural privilege of offering Christ's perfect sacrifice. We receive the Lord in the Eucharist, and by that communion he also receives us. These are some of the most important activities we will ever do.

Because the Mass unites us with God and with each other, families should worship together at the Sunday liturgy. It's a chance to build our family unity and celebrate it in the Lord's presence. I recommend that parents make it a policy that whoever lives at home worships with the family at Sunday Mass. For thirty years our family has benefited from this practice. Being together around the altar has given us grace and wisdom for being together around the house.

Worshiping with children is not easy, and I would not want to give you an over-spiritual view of it. Infants and toddlers may be fussy, younger children may not be able to pay attention, and older children may be bored. Caring for kids at Mass can be so distracting as to make parents wonder whether it's worth the effort.

But parents must not expect the Sunday liturgy to be an occasion for personal devotion or quiet meditation. Mass is a corporate activity of the body of Christ that we share in. We don't need to feel very good about it. While comforting infants, refereeing grade schoolers, and waking teens who claim to be meditating, we can still worship quite well enough to please God, even though we might not be pleased ourselves.

Worshiping together at Mass can play a significant role in forming our kids in the faith. So we should not relax the policy except for good reasons. In our family, for example, we may make an exception for teenagers who want to worship at Mass with their Catholic friends.

Every family might not be able to worship together, as in situations where one parent is not Catholic or is not practicing his or her faith. In many of these cases, the nonparticipating parent will agree to support, or at least not to oppose, the active parent in expecting the rest of the family to attend Sunday Mass together.

Older teens sometimes rebel and refuse to attend Mass with the family. Often their real issue is not Mass or religion, but tension in family relationships or other personal problems. Caring for a child in these circumstances may require parents to suspend their Mass attendance policy. Forcing it may even drive a wedge between the teen and God. Better now to rely on prayer, love, and counsel to resolve the bigger problems, and get them back to Mass when the situation has improved.

❦

Mothers, do you teach your children the Christian prayers? Do you prepare them . . . for the sacraments? Fathers, do you pray with your children? Your example of honesty in thought and action, joined to some common prayer, is a lesson for life, an act of worship of singular value.

Pope Paul VI

For Discussion

• Why should families worship together at Mass?
• Under what circumstances might parents relax their expectations that kids attend Mass with the family?
• What should a parent do about family Mass attendance when the other parent is nonparticipating?

For Reflection

• Does my family worship together at Sunday Mass? Why or why not?
• If not, what can I do about it? If yes, what can I do to improve our experience of family worship?

Application Ideas

• Consider making Sunday worship together a regular feature of your family's life. If possible, make Sunday worship together a family policy. Here are some tips for taking that step:
  - Study and review your reasons for wanting to worship together as a family.
  - Prepare the family by instructing the children about the Mass and the value of Sunday worship together.
  - Explain the policy and your reasons for it.
  - Look for continuing opportunities to speak with the children about the importance and benefits of worshiping at Mass.

Resources

Catechism of the Catholic Church, nos. 2174-2195.
Pope John Paul II, *On the Family* (Washington, D.C.: United States Catholic Conference, 202-541-3090), 59-62.
Bert Ghezzi, *Keeping Your Kids Catholic* (Servant Publications: 1-800-458-8505), chapter 5.

12 Let Scripture Surprise You

❧ *When we read the Bible together as a family, the Holy Spirit will help us lead our children to the Lord.*

And the Word became flesh and dwelt among us. John 1:14

Once a religion teacher asked my youngest daughter, Mary, to name her favorite Bible verse. Mary immediately picked the pearl of great price parable (Matthew 13:45). I think she chose that verse because the way we interpreted it at a family prayer time made her feel loved. We turned the parable around, saying that God was the pearl merchant who gave up everything for love of us, his pearls of great price. I also think she chose it because we had just read it the night before.

That scenario might not have happened just a generation ago. Before Vatican Council II, most Catholic families did not read Scripture at home and they heard very little Scripture at church because Mass was in Latin.

The reform of the liturgy since Vatican II has played a big part in reviving the interest of Catholics in the Bible. Now at Mass during the liturgy of the Word, we meet the Lord and hear his voice in the proclamation of Scripture. Jesus does not restrict his presence to the Eucharist, for he is also present in his Word. That's why we treat the gospel book with such reverence.

The reading of God's Word at Mass has drawn our attention to the importance of Scripture for our Christian lives. As a result, many Catholics have made reading the Bible together a regular family activity.

Parents don't need to be Bible scholars or catechists to read Scripture with their children. Right now our kids need to hear the Word of God. They can learn to dissect it later on. When we come across something that stumps us, plenty of help is available in good books.

We also don't need to be afraid that our kids will react negatively. When parents open the Bible and plunge in with the family, they find to their surprise that the children like it. Reading Scripture has its own appeal because the Holy Spirit is at work when we do it, touching big and little hearts alike.

Reading the Scriptures from the Sunday liturgy sometime before or after Mass is an easy way to get started. I recommend beginning with the gospel, and choosing one of the other readings only when it is especially appropriate.

But families can take other approaches to reading Scripture. Here are a few suggestions.

For families with very young children, parents should use Bible story books or videos.

Families with children in the lower grades should try a series of selected short New Testament passages, like the parable that captivated my daughter. Parents can begin to use longer selections and whole books with older children. Start with the Sermon on the Mount (Matthew 5:1—7:28) and move on to the gospel of Mark.

We should marshal as much effort as we can to build Scripture reading into our family routine. Like worshiping together at Mass, I think reading Scripture as a family is a key way for parents to hand on the faith to their children.

❦

May the Lord Jesus touch our eyes
as he did those of the blind.
Then we shall begin to see
in visible things those which are invisible.

Origen

For Discussion
• How has liturgical renewal awakened interest in Bible study?
• Why should families read Scripture together?

For Reflection
• Do I read Scripture regularly? What could I do differently to improve my study of Scripture?
• Do we read Scripture together as a family?

Application Ideas

- Consider how you could start the practice of Bible reading in your family. Figure out the best approach by reviewing the circumstances and needs of your family. Select one of the approaches recommended in this article, or develop your own plan.
- If you already read Scripture together, review what you are doing to determine if you could do something to improve your approach.

Resources

Catechism of the Catholic Church, nos. 131-133.

The Eager Reader Bible Story Book (Our Sunday Visitor: 1-800-348-2440).

Jim Auer, *A Teenager's (Absolutely Basic) Introduction to the New Testament* (Liguori Publications: 1-800-325-9521, ext. 657).

Alfred McBride, O. Praem., *Our Sunday Visitor's Popular Bible Study* (set of six New Testament study books; Our Sunday Visitor: 1-800-348-2440).

Bill Dodds, *Bedtime Parables* (Our Sunday Visitor: 1-800-348-2440).

13 Teaching Your Children to Pray

❦ *Conversations with the Lord help children become aware of God's presence and get to know him personally.*

Rejoice always, pray constantly, give thanks in all circumstances. 1 Thessalonians 5:16

One of the lessons I learned in early childhood was that God was a person who was present in our home and who loved me. My mother accomplished this by teaching me the traditional Catholic prayers and by giving good example: Every night she knelt at her bedside to pray. These simple things were enough to make me aware of the Lord.

Our responsibility to hand on the faith to our children can overwhelm us if we try to accomplish too many things. But if we put a few essentials in place, they will give our families a Catholic orientation and have a life-shaping effect on our kids. Among these essentials are worshiping together at Mass, having a family prayer time, talking to our children about our relationship with God, and teaching them to pray. Activities like these make our supernatural lives down-to-earth realities for us and for our children.

If we never speak to the Lord, we can go through our daily routines without noticing him, even though he is right there loving us. But talking to him in prayer recognizes his presence and draws him into our lives. So teaching our children to pray makes it clear to them that God is a person who is near and interested in them. When they tell the Lord their needs or give him thanks, they are acknowledging him and reaching out to touch him.

We should approach teaching our kids to pray the same way we teach them hygiene — as a normal part of life, something we do everyday because our spiritual health depends on it. Here are some tips that you will find helpful:

- Begin to pray with your children as early as possible in their lives, even when they are still in the womb. Bless them morning and night with the sign of the cross to invoke the grace of their baptisms.

- Worshiping together at Mass and having a regular family prayer time are important activities that create a family prayer tradition. There's no better way to teach kids to pray than by praying.
- As soon as they are able, have small children memorize traditional prayers. Be sure your list includes the Our Father, the Apostles' Creed, the Hail Mary, and an act of contrition. Help the children pray these prayers at bedtime, and use them regularly in family prayer.
- Take the time to explain the meaning of the prayers so that the children can pray them from the heart. Every night my mother had me pray the child's bedtime prayer, "Now I lay me down to sleep." I think I was eight years old before I figured out that "Afashadai" meant "If I should die."
- Teach the children to talk to the Lord in their own words. Help them thank the Lord for good things and to ask his help for needs and problems. Of course, the best way to teach conversational prayer is to set an example in the family.
- Encourage older children to take a brief daily prayer time. Help them select a book of prayers or meditations aimed at youth. Environment is important to teens, so be open to their finding a special place to pray where they can light candles or play musical instruments.

And get in the habit of daily prayer yourself. You want to give your children an example that they can imitate.

❧

Your informal conversation is actually the most important of all factors in the religious education of your children. . . . The way you talk during ordinary family life, about the house or at table, counts most. If you speak often and naturally about God, his power, wisdom and goodness; if you explain all joys, sorrows and problems of life in terms of God's lordship and providence . . . then your children will learn from you the most vital of all lessons — that God comes first. Of course if you drag these subjects in artificially to impress the children, then your talk will not ring true

and they will sense it. But if God and the things of God are really the prime interest of your own lives, then they will also fill the lives of your children.

Clifford Howell, S.J.

For Discussion

• How does personal prayer affect our relationship with God?

For Reflection

• Do all family members know and pray the traditional Catholic prayers? If not, what step can I take to help them learn these prayers?

Application Ideas

• Consider the relationship of each of your children to the Lord. Ask yourself questions like:
   - What is my child's relationship to the Lord?
   - Does he or she seem to know God as a person?
   - Has my child learned the traditional prayers?
   - How does my child participate in Sunday worship and family prayer?
   - After reviewing the relationship of a child to the Lord, consider what you could do to help your child grow closer to him.

Resources

Catechism of the Catholic Church, nos. 2228; 2745; 2685; 2691.

Mary Ann Kuharski, *Parenting With Prayer* (Our Sunday Visitor: 1-800-348-2440).

Bert Ghezzi, *Keeping Your Kids Catholic* (Servant Publications: 1-800-458-8505), chapters 5 and 6.

A Catholic Prayer Book (Our Sunday Visitor: 1-800-348-2440).

The Catholic Prayer Book (Servant Publications: 1-800-458-8505).

14 Living the Year With Christ

🍂 *Every year the Church celebrates the life of Christ*
sacramentally so that we can live more fully in him.

It is no longer I who live, but Christ who lives in me; and the
life I now live in the flesh I live by faith in the Son of God,
who loved me and gave himself for me. Galatians 2:20

One of our early family Christmas celebrations was unforgettable.
We had the children dramatize the first Christmas. Stephen, age one,
was the infant Jesus and Elaine, age three, was Mary. The two oldest
boys were Joseph and a shepherd. When the Christ Child began to
squirm noisily, our little Virgin Mary slammed him to the coffee table
manger, shouting, "Lay down, baby Jesus, lay down!"

Without a sense of humor and the willingness to try again after
failure, my wife and I would have abandoned our attempts to develop
Christian family customs. But because we felt strongly that we had to
do something to link our Sunday worship with family life, we kept
working at it.

The Church celebrates the life of Christ throughout the year. From
Advent, when we anticipate Christ's birth and second coming to the
feast of Christ the King, when we exalt his glory, the liturgy presents
the life of Jesus as a pattern for us. In word and sacrament, the Church
provides the acts of Christ that bring us salvation.

Our response is to conform ever more closely to his life by
applying sacramental graces to our lives. To do this we cannot restrict
our participation in Christ's life to Sunday Mass, which, I think, is
limiting ourselves to a sacramental half-life. To live fully in Christ, we
must live with him at home.

Families should develop customs that help them live the years with
Christ. These practices serve as prompts that lead us to respond to the
Lord, making our lives more like his. They also catch the attention of
our kids and help to draw them to the things of God. From the many
possibilities, we should select practices that work best for our families.

Some of our family choices over thirty years included: the Advent wreath, the Christmas tree blessing, a gala Christmas-Eve party, an Epiphany procession, simple Lenten meals, the Passover Meal, participation in the Easter Vigil, and an extra-special Easter breakfast.

We had some rules of thumb for creating our family customs. You may also find them helpful. Family customs should be:

Simple. A simple custom delivers a clear message and is easy to do. The more complex things are, the more likely we are to postpone or skip them when we get busy. Our simplest practice is a family favorite — the Easter morning search for the golden alleluia egg. The finder gets a gift to share with all.

Relational. Look for practices that help family members grow in loving each other. For example, for Advent have everyone draw another's name, and do an act of kindness for the person every day before Christmas.

Focused outward. In your mix of customs, include some that reach out to others. For example, invite a guest to Christmas or Easter dinner, or give money saved by Lenten fasting to a needy family. Something like volunteering an afternoon at a soup kitchen at Easter time can have a life-shaping effect on a child.

Fun. While some activities may be appropriately serious, the majority of our customs should be enjoyable. We want to communicate the joy of Christian living to our kids.

Consistent. As we evolve our family customs, we should see that we do them consistently every year. They play an important role in the Christian formation of our children, and they also help create a sense of unity and identity in the family. The first time, for example, that we failed to have the search for the golden alleluia egg, a twenty-year-old son complained. Maybe he just wanted another chance to find it, since he never had before. But I think that he realized that abandoning the custom would be a loss to the family.

❦

The sacraments are Jesus' way of humanizing the spiritual, adapting it to the manner of human beings. In talking to a little child, you use simple words and short sentences suited to his understanding. . . . You don't merely speak, you *show* him what

you mean. Similarly the sacraments are used by Christ to communicate in a way that speaks to our whole nature. Even children can understand them.

Edward D. O'Connor, C.S.C.

For Discussion
• Why should we celebrate the year with Christ at home?

For Reflection
• How do I respond to the life of Christ that the Church presents in the liturgical seasons? What do I do to apply the liturgy to my life?

Application Ideas
• Review your family customs for the main seasons and feasts of the liturgical year. Determine whether they are complete and effective. Ask the following questions:
  - Do the children understand why we have family customs? Do they understand the purpose of each custom? How can we increase their understanding?
  - Do we use our family customs consistently every year? If not, how can we ensure that we will be more consistent in the future?
  - Is there a major season or feast for which we have no family customs? If yes, what could we do to celebrate that season or feast?
  - Should we replace any of our current customs? What should we do differently?

Resources
Catechism of the Catholic Church, nos. 1095; 1168-1173; 1194.

Many publishers offer books and pamphlets to help families celebrate the liturgical year. Use the telephone numbers listed in the appendix to request their catalogs.

Empowered for Personal Growth

> **"** *Let us become like unto Christ,*
> *Since Christ became like unto us.*
> *Let us become gods for his sake,*
> *Since he became human for ours.* **"**

St. Gregory Nazianzen

15 The Christian Growth Wheel

❦ *Prayer, study, service, and fellowship are four essentials that transmit the power of the sacraments to our lives.*

As therefore you received Christ Jesus the Lord, so live in him, rooted and built up in him and established in the faith. Colossians 2:6-7

The Lord designed the sacraments to affect the way we live. They put us in Christ so that we have the power to live our ordinary lives in extraordinary ways. This power is God's free gift, so we don't have to work at getting it. But we do have to work at applying it. To help us do this, the Lord has given us four essential practices that bring grace into action. They are prayer, study, service, and fellowship.

An image of a wheel shows how these activities tap the power of the sacraments for daily Christian living. Christ is at the hub of the wheel, releasing the energy of the Holy Spirit for us. The rim represents our daily lives. Our job is to get Christ's power from the hub to the rim. We do this through prayer, study, service, and fellowship, which are the four spokes of the wheel. When they are all functioning properly, our Christian lives move ahead surely.

So to live Christ-empowered lives, we must pay attention to these four areas:

Prayer. Prayer activates our participation in the divine life that the Lord gives us in baptism, confirmation, and the Eucharist. He has made us members of his family, but we will not come to know him better unless we communicate with him. So to live fully in Christ, we must spend some time in prayer every day.

Consider these suggestions to help you start or strengthen daily personal prayer:

- Pick a time of day that you can routinely spend in prayer and a place where you feel comfortable praying.
- Try to choose a prime time because you want to be alert when speaking with God.

- Start with five or ten minutes at most, but be open to taking more time as you become more experienced.
- Make use of tools that can help you pray — traditional prayers, the Bible, psalms, prayer books, the rosary, a hymnal.
- Be sure to talk personally to the Lord and to intercede for yourself and your family.

Study. What we think has a big effect on what we do. The more we know God and understand his ways, the more we can please him. Study increases our knowledge and understanding. Reading the Bible and good Christian literature gives us:

- Information about God, his plan, and his people.
- Practical wisdom for living.
- Insight into Christian truths.
- Greater personal knowledge of God.

Like prayer, study channels grace into our lives, giving the Holy Spirit a chance to inspire us with truths that change us.

Service. The commandment to love others sums up Jesus' message. It heads the list of his teachings and covers everything. Service is the way we express our Christian love, for Christ called all of us to imitate his love by serving the needs of our neighbors. Here are some of the many ways that we can perform Christian service every day:

- We care for each other in our families and living situations.
- We put the interests of others ahead of our own.
- We meet the material and spiritual needs of others.
- We are active in our parishes.
- We spend time in social action and working to change social structures.
- We speak and act in ways that help others find Christ and the Church.

The Holy Spirit fills us with the love of God (Romans 5:5) and our service puts that love into action.

Fellowship. By design, Christianity is a community. It is the family of God's children. The Father wants us to express our love for him by loving our brothers and sisters. Through the sacraments, the local community gives us our Christian lives. Now as members of the community, we share our lives. The Lord does not intend us to tough out our Christian journey alone. He wants us to enjoy the support we find in the Christian community. Consider these opportunities for fellowship:

- Share your Christian life openly in your family or living situation.
- With your spouse or a few friends, regularly review your Christian growth — your prayer, study, service, and fellowship.
- Participate actively in a parish service, support group, outreach, or organization.
- Take part in a Bible study or prayer group.
- Work in a social action or evangelization program.

When you pay attention to any area it goes better. This truism from business applies equally well to the Christian life. Paying attention to the four essentials of Christian growth helps us bring grace to life.

❧

God will not judge us on our earthly possessions and human success, but on how much we have loved.

St. John of the Cross

For Discussion

- Explain how each of the four Christian growth essentials applies the grace of the sacraments to everyday living.

For Reflection

- Use the Christian growth wheel to review your Christian life. What could you do differently to improve in each area?

Application Ideas

- Choose one of the four essentials that is most important to you and decide to do one thing to make it work better in your life.
- Use the growth wheel to teach children about the Christian essentials. Have fellowship with them by sharing openly about your Christian lives. Teach them to pray. Study with them. Look for simple and manageable ways to involve them in service.

Resources

Catechism of the Catholic Church, nos. 141; 2743-2745; 2653-2654.
New Covenant (monthly magazine about spiritual renewal; Our Sunday Visitor: 1-800-348-2440).

16 Prime Time for the Lord

❧ *Daily prayer is an essential of Christian growth because it releases the energy of the Holy Spirit in us.*

O Lord, open . . . my lips, and my mouth shall show forth thy praise. Psalm 51:15

About the time a child turns thirteen parents commonly observe that silence falls, like the heavy velvet curtain at the end of a play. All of a sudden, it seems, our wonderful little chatterboxes clam up and rarely speak to us. Without much conversation, the parent-child relationship seems to grow distant and may become strained.

I think that's the way it can be between us and God, our Father, when we are not praying regularly. He starts the conversation by telling us that he loves us. Then he waits patiently for us to say something. We do talk to him occasionally, usually when we need something or are having a problem. But if we are not talking to him often, we are not keeping up our part of the relationship.

Human beings understand intuitively that relationships require a substantial investment of time. Close friends and lovers expect to talk to each other frequently even when they live miles apart. My three oldest sons' monthly phone bills will serve as evidence. We should not be surprised that maintaining our relationship with the Lord, the most important relationship of all, takes daily conversation.

Daily prayer is an essential means of Christian growth. It activates our participation in the life of the Spirit, which we can let lie dormant if we do not stir it by talking with the Lord. Most of us prefer steak on the grill to steak in the freezer. It's the same with the Holy Spirit — we can keep him frozen or have him on fire, and daily prayer makes the difference.

Many of us snatch chances to pray during our daily routines. That's good, but its not enough. To build our friendship with God, we need to give some of our best time to speaking with him. We must set aside prime time for the Lord. To do this we may have to make some adjustments; for example, going to bed earlier so we can get up fifteen minutes before the family or arranging for our spouse to cover for us while we pray. Whatever it takes, it's worth doing to strengthen our divine relationship.

We don't need to worry about what we will talk to the Lord about. He wants to hear what's on our heart, and our hearts are usually full of things we need to say or to discuss with him. The best approach is to start our prayer time by inviting the Holy Spirit to inspire and guide our prayer. With the psalmist we can pray, "O Lord open . . . my lips, and my mouth shall show forth thy praise."

All prayer falls into four categories — praise, thanksgiving, repentance, and petition, and thinking about these areas can help us carry on our conversations with God. Depending on what's happening in our lives, we can begin with any one of these and move to the others:

- We can start our prayer with praise and thanksgiving, perhaps using a psalm to stimulate our thoughts and to prime us for spontaneous worship.
- We can use the Lord's Prayer to help us confess our desire to conform to the Father's will and to repent of behavior patterns that lead us away from him.
- We can approach the Lord confidently and ask him for whatever we need. Remember that the more we pray for what is on the Lord's heart, the more we can expect God to say yes. That's what it means to pray in Jesus' name (John 14:13-14). So I always pray for the salvation of my family and friends, expecting God to act because I know that's something he desires even more than I do.

Since prayer is a conversation, we should be sure to spend some time listening to God. He may have been waiting a while to say a few things to us.

I hear from within me, as from a spring of living water, the murmur: "Come to the Father."

St. Ignatius of Antioch

For Discussion

• Why is personal prayer an essential means of Christian growth?
• How can the four categories of prayer help us to pray spontaneously?

For Reflection:

• Do I set aside prime time daily for prayer? If yes, what one thing could I do differently to improve my prayer? If not, what can I do differently to fit a prayer time into my daily routine?

Application Ideas

• If you do not have a regular daily prayer time, consider starting one. Take time to plan it well so that you get off to a good beginning. Especially look for the right time and place and figure out what you must do to stay faithful to the prayer time.
• Consider praying psalms as part of your personal prayer time and at family prayer. Encourage family members to use them as well. Start with the following psalms that correspond to the four types of prayer:
    Psalm 148 (Praise)
    Psalm 116 (Thanksgiving)
    Psalm 51 (Repentance)
    Psalm 6 (Petition)

Resources

Catechism of the Catholic Church, nos. 2626-2643.

Lord Hear Our Prayer (Ave Maria Press: 1-800-282-1865).

Eamon Tobin, *Prayer: A Handbook for Today's Catholic* (Liguori Publications: 1-800-325-9521, ext. 651).

Thomas H. Green, *Opening to God* (Ave Maria Press: 1-800-282-1865).

Mary Ann Kuharski, *How to Talk to Your Children About Prayer* (Our Sunday Visitor: 1-800-348-2440).

17 Read for Your Life

 *Study is essential for Christian growth because it leads to knowledge of God and works with grace to sanctify us.*

Make every effort to supplement your faith with virtue, and virtue with knowledge, and knowledge with self-control. 2 Peter 1:5-6

At the end of a shelf in my office is a collection of books that I prize because they changed my life in some way. Standing shoulder to shoulder there are some unlikely companions: C. S. Lewis's *The Screwtape Letters*, David Wilkerson's *The Cross and the Switchblade*, Garrett Mattingly's *Catherine of Aragon*, and Plato's *Meno*, to name a few.

Also among my life-changing books is Frank Sheed's *Theology and Sanity*, where I learned that my sanity depended on recognizing spiritual realities that many humans ignore to their peril. I value my little treasury of books because each contributed to my spiritual health by fixing some truth in my mind, by expanding my perspective on reality or by getting me to alter my behavior — the latter being an accomplishment of staggering proportions. Just ask my long-suffering wife.

Sometimes when we are reading for pleasure or information, we get more than we expected. We may be just browsing for knowledge about things and be surprised to discover knowledge that makes us better. Not only do our minds get enlightened, but occasionally a truth shoots straight from our brains to our hearts and charges our wills to act.

That's why study is an essential of Christian growth. We read Scripture and Christian books to understand more about God, his ways, and the Church. The truths we find throw light on our paths and help us keep our journey on the right track. They work along with sacramental graces to transform us, prompting us to behave more like Christ.

So we must read for our lives, and the book that our life depends on is the Bible. Because Scripture is the revealed word of God, it is unlike every other book. When we are studying any other book, we cannot speak to the author and the author cannot speak to us. But the Bible, like a sacrament, is a door to the sacred. It takes us into God's presence. When we read God's word, we meet the Author in person. He speaks directly to us with words he inspired in human writers centuries ago. And we can speak directly to him. Reading Scripture expands our knowledge about God's ways, but even better, it increases our knowledge of God himself.

We should be reading other Christian literature, too — the great Christian writers, books old and new, Catholic magazines, newspapers, pamphlets, and so on. The Church has traditionally called this kind of study "spiritual reading" because it opens us to the influence of the Holy Spirit. It's the activity of the Spirit that transforms our study into discovery. He takes a truth we thought we had down pat and turns it into a revolutionary principle that can radically alter our ways of thinking and acting. That's what he has done repeatedly to me. Most recently, for example, he revitalized my understanding and experience of the supernatural life, the body of Christ, and the power of sacramental signs through my reading of Clifford Howell's classic, *Of Sacraments and Sacrifice.*

We may recognize big gaps in our Christian education and feel that we don't know where to begin to fill them. If that's your situation, ask the Holy Spirit to guide you in selecting Scripture and other material that will help you grow in Christ. Let me suggest two New Testament books that are good starters: the gospel of Mark and the first letter of Peter.

Growing in knowledge of God is a lifelong activity, longer than life, really, since we'll spend eternity getting to know him in his inexhaustible greatness. But now is the time to get started.

❦

Reading Scripture is not like taking one's wife out to dinner on special occasions; it must be like the evening supper that husband and wife share, day in, day out. . . . Just as our daily supper nourishes us, our daily reading of Scripture will bring the strength of God into our everyday lives. Anything less than daily reading is likely to lead to spiritual malnutrition.

George Martin

For Discussion

• Why is study an essential for Christian growth?
• In what ways can study change us?

For Reflection

• On what occasions has study led me to discover a life-changing truth? Do I read Scripture regularly? Do I read other kinds of Christian literature?

Application Ideas

• Make all your study "spiritual reading" by saying a prayer to the Holy Spirit for guidance each time before you start reading.
• Review your study habits to determine how well you utilize this essential means of Christian growth. What could you do differently to improve your study?
• By word and example, parents must teach their children the importance of study as a means of Christian growth. Here are some suggestions:
   - Read Bible stories, simplified lives of the saints, and other good books to your children. Continue the practice as kids get older, reading the gospels and books like C. S. Lewis's *The Narnia Chronicles.*
   - When children have learned to read, consider establishing a family reading hour from 7 to 8 p.m. or whatever period works best for your family. Help the children select the books they will read at that time. Provide a popular children's Bible and other good books at home, but also make use of parish and public libraries. Family reading hour is not only an introduction to the habit of study, but it is also a great replacement for an hour of prime-time television.

Resources

Catechism of the Catholic Church, nos. 141; 2743-2745.
George Martin, *Reading Scripture as the Word of God* (Servant Publications: 1-800-458-8505).
Catholic Family-Time Bible Stories in Pictures (Our Sunday Visitor: 1-800-348-2440).

18 Doing Things Differently With Scripture

Four questions can help us figure out the meaning of Scripture and apply it.

Every one then who hears these words of mine and does them will be like a wise man who built his house upon the rock. Matthew 7:24

Even though we share in God's life, many things about us don't appear to be very divine. A goal of the Christian life is to change that fact so that we become more like the Lord. Paul says that we have replaced our old nature with a new nature "which is being renewed in knowledge after the image of its creator" (Colossians 3:10).

The Lord has given us the sacraments and Scripture as means for our transformation in Christ. The sacraments are sources of life-changing grace. Through them the Holy Spirit gives us the strength to say no to our bad desires and yes to the good conduct God wants.

Scripture works along with the sacraments for our transformation by giving us a picture of the behavior the Lord expects. The sacraments give us outpourings of the Holy Spirit, who supports us in changing our behavior and transforming our lives. But we must work at understanding Scripture to find out what God's will is before we can conform to it.

Four questions can help us figure out the meaning of Scripture and apply it to our lives. We can use them when we reflect on Scripture we hear proclaimed at Mass or read it together as a family. They are:

- What was the original writer saying?
- What is the Lord saying to me now?
- What difference does it make?
- What can I do differently?

In the Bible, the Lord spoke to us through human writers. The first step to understanding God's message is to determine what the writer was trying to communicate. To get at the meaning of a text we must ask, "What was the original writer saying?" We must know things like his purpose, his recipients, and his circumstances. For example, we will get more out of 1 Peter if we recognize that it was written for Christians like us, who were "aliens" in their societies because their ideals put them out of step with their world.

The Bible is different from every other book because its divine author actively speaks through it. If we are not attentive to the Spirit, we will miss the greater part of what the Lord wants to communicate to us. So we must always ask, "What is the Lord saying to me now?"

Asking "What difference does it make?" helps us to identify specific ways in which our behavior does not conform to God's will. Suppose that we are comparing our conduct to this verse: "Practice hospitality ungrudgingly to one another" (1 Peter 4:9). We should ask how our practice differs from this precept. Spin-off questions will pop into our minds: Do I welcome people into my home? Do I lend things freely? And so on.

Once we recognize how we vary from the biblical norm, we can begin to conform to it more closely by asking, "What can I do differently?" For example, if the answer to the previous question is that I rarely lend anything to people when asked, I can use this question to decide how to change. Considering what I can do differently will suggest numerous possible steps I could take to improve my hospitality. From these options I should choose the one that will bring me closest to complying with the standard.

Then, of course, comes the hardest part — doing it. But being able to figure out what I must do differently to become more like the Lord is a big step forward.

❧

Holy Scripture is the table of Christ, where we are nourished, where we learn what we should love and what we should desire, to whom we should have our eyes raised.

Alcuin of York

For Discussion

• How do the sacraments and Scripture work together to help us become more like Christ? Why does sound Scripture interpretation require our understanding what the original writer intended? Why must we seek what the Spirit is saying to us now?

For Reflection

• What kind of a response do I make to Scripture? Do I try to apply it to my life?
• How could we use the four questions for understanding to help family members hear God and apply Scripture to their lives?

Application Ideas

• Scripture study is an imperative for growth in Christ, so adult Christians should make regular time for it. Examine the patterns of your daily life, looking for a way to spend a few minutes reading and reflecting on God's Word.
  - Start with a gospel or one of the New Testament letters like 1 Peter or Colossians.
  - Use the four questions presented in this article.

Resources

God's Word Today (A monthly magazine that presents daily reflections on Bible books and themes); George Martin, editor, P.O. Box 64090, St. Paul, MN 55164.

Alfred McBride, O. Praem., *Our Sunday Visitor's Popular Bible Study* (set of six New Testament study books; Our Sunday Visitor: 1-800-348-2440).

19 <u>Improving Your Service</u>

🦋 *The Holy Spirit gives us a wide assortment of spiritual gifts that equip us to serve others.*

"I am among you as one who serves." Luke 22:27

Jesus designed the Church so that it would not only continue his ministry, but that it would also substantially increase his service to humankind. In his physical body, Jesus was limited to caring for people in Galilee and Judea, which were relatively tiny places. But now through us, his disciples in the body of Christ, he reaches beyond all geographical boundaries to minister to people everywhere. Our participation in this service is not an optional extra. It is an essential means for applying the Lord's grace to real-life situations.

The sacraments are power sources in the body of Christ that equip us for service. Baptism and confirmation give us the Holy Spirit, who dispenses a wide assortment of gifts among the members of the body. His gifts enable us to put love in action and meet our neighbors' material and spiritual needs.

Confirmation dispenses seven gifts of the Spirit that deepen our relationship to God. (See Isaiah 11:2.) Wisdom, knowledge, understanding, and counsel supernaturally increase our knowledge of God. Fortitude, piety, and fear of the Lord dispose us to obey him. These gifts strengthen us to serve by grounding us firmly in the Lord:

- Wisdom gives us insight into God's ways.
- Understanding increases our grasp of the Christian mysteries.
- Counsel equips us to discern and avoid spiritual obstacles.
- Knowledge reveals the will of God in our lives.
- Fortitude empowers us to obey the Lord even in difficulties.
- Fear of the Lord convinces us of God's authority.
- Piety sets our hearts aflame with devotion to God.

The Holy Spirit also brings us numerous spiritual gifts of service, called charisms. (See 1 Corinthians 12:4-11.) These gifts help us build up the Church so that it can carry on Christ's ministry more effectively. They also help us bring new life and mercy to the world around us. They include gifts like wisdom that shows us what to do, prophecy that gives us God's words to speak, and healing that brings relief and health to the sick. In effect, the Holy Spirit makes of each of us a gift to the people near us, with unique and valuable services to perform for them.

We don't need to spend a lot of time figuring out what our gifts are before we start to serve. That kind of thinking only postpones action. What our gifts are will become apparent once we have spent a little time working with Christ.

Here are some tips for starting or improving your service:

- Our mission as Christians is to help others find Christ and the Church. So we can perform our main service every day by speaking and acting in ways that move people nearer to the Lord.
- Consider the needs of the people in your immediate social environments — family, work, parish, school, and so on. Decide to meet one or two of the needs you identify.
- Some of our service should be personal, done for people with names and faces because caring for people is the essence of Christianity.
- We should only undertake services that fit with our state in life, existing commitments and time constraints. For example, it is probably unwise to add on a service that takes three evenings a week and Saturdays to a full family- and work-schedule. Something has to give, so we will soon abandon the service, fail in our primary commitments, or burn out in trying to do everything.
- When looking for ways to serve, we should consult the clues given by our inclinations and natural abilities. Sometimes the strong desire we have to do something is the Holy Spirit's leading. And grace builds on nature, so that if we are naturally good at something, it may be that the Lord wants to inspire us and direct us in using that natural gift in his service.

❦

I have placed you in the midst of your fellows so that you may do to them what you cannot do to me, that is to say, that you may love

your neighbor freely without expecting any return from him, and what you do to him I count as done to me.

St. Catherine of Siena

For Discussion

• Why is service not optional, but essential for Christians?
• How do the gifts of the Holy Spirit equip us for service?

For Reflection

• In what ways am I already performing Christian service? At home? At work? In my parish? In other situations?
• Are there some other ways in which I should be serving?
• What one thing could I do differently to improve my Christian service?

Application Ideas

• Review your involvement in Christian service. Make a list of all the things you are doing and consider them in light of the tips above. Identify the ways you could improve your service, and consider doing one or two of them.
• Involving children in service is an important way to help them grow close to Christ and to find themselves at home in the Church. Look for some simple and manageable service that you can do along with your child. Consider possibilities like these:
  - Serving sick or elderly neighbors by providing them transportation to doctors or church or by doing yard work or housework for them.
  - Volunteering for several hours a month at a hospital or social service program.
  - Doing child care for a single parent, or providing "big brothers" or "big sisters" for his or her children.

Resources

Catechism of the Catholic Church, nos. 798-801; 2003.
Virgil Gulker, *Helping You Is Helping Me* (Servant Publications: 1-800-458-8505).

20 Give Away Your Faith

❧ *We can share our faith by acting and speaking in ways that nudge family and friends closer to the Lord.*

"Go therefore and make disciples of all nations, baptizing them in the name of the Father and of the Son and of the Holy Spirit, teaching them to observe all that I have commanded you; and lo, I am with you always, to the close of the age." Matthew 28:19-20

Christianity is built on a principle that contradicts our natural human tendency to selfishness. We are inclined to get things for ourselves and to go after more. But Jesus taught that if we wanted to gain our lives — the most important thing of all — we must lose them for him and for the gospel. (See Mark 8:35.)

This paradoxical principle of giving everything to gain even more pervades the Christian way. Jesus taught, for example, that our love bears much fruit when we spend ourselves unselfishly serving others. (See John 15:11-17.) The Lord arranged that our love would grow enormously if we give it freely. The same is true for faith. Few things strengthen faith more than sharing it with friends and seeing them respond by giving their lives to God.

The Lord designed the Church so that it would add members one at a time and person to person. That's how he implemented his Father's plan in his ministry and that's how he expects us to continue his work. Baptism makes us collaborators with Christ in bringing others to the Father so that he can give them new life in the Spirit. "No believer in Christ," said Pope John Paul II, "can avoid this supreme duty to proclaim Christ to all peoples." So we are obliged to share our faith with others.

Bearing witness to Christ and the Church may seem difficult. Fear or other obstacles may prevent us from telling others about our relationship with God. But the Lord is with us to help us give our faith away. The Holy Spirit we received in baptism impels us to do it and guides all our efforts. We sense his promptings most clearly in our desires to see our children, relatives, and close friends find final salvation in the Lord.

Sharing our faith mainly means acting and speaking in ways that draw people to Christ. By serving people in ways that make them feel loved, we intrigue them and nudge them closer to the Lord. A family member senses our love, for example, when we do unexpected acts of kindness like doing a household chore or putting gasoline in a spouse's car. This past year a colleague at work made me feel loved by providing a meal for my family when she heard my wife had injured her back. We can all do such things in the course of our daily routines.

But the time will come when we must talk. In sharing our faith, actions are not a substitute for words. St. Peter said that we should always be ready to give an explanation to anyone who asks why we have hope (1 Peter 3:15). When people ask questions or give us openings, we should take the opportunity to tell them about our relationship with the Lord. We don't need to make fancy speeches or display exquisite familiarity with Scripture. We just need to tell them in our own words what the Lord has done for us and why we love him. The Holy Spirit will take it from there.

I have found it helpful to have a little agreement with myself to take a few simple steps to ensure that I am sharing my faith. I commit myself to:

- Pray for my family, friends, and associates.
- Do things for them that they will perceive as love.
- Take opportunities to tell them what the Lord has done for me.

Holding myself to these guidelines keeps me aware of my part in helping others find Christ and the Church, and overcomes any inertia that might keep me from giving away my faith.

🍒

All Christ's faithful have the obligation and the right to strive so that the divine message of salvation may more and more reach all people of all times and all places.

Code of Canon Law, 211

For Discussion

• Why can it be said that faith increases when we share it with others?
• Why must sharing faith always involve both actions and words?

For Reflection

• In what ways do I help people close to me draw nearer to God? Am I prepared to tell others about my relationship with him?

Application Ideas

• If you do not already pray daily for your family, friends, and associates, consider how you can start.
• Prepare yourself to give an explanation of your faith to anyone who gives you an opening. Reflect on what the Lord has done for you so that you can give a brief witness when the opportunity presents itself.
• Teach family members that sharing faith means acting and speaking in ways that help people draw nearer to the Lord. Get children started by encouraging them to practice acts of kindness for their siblings and friends. Explain that it's the Holy Spirit who prompts and directs such actions. This lays a foundation for their being able to speak to others about the Lord as their own faith grows.

Resources

Bert Ghezzi, *Sharing Your Faith: A User's Guide to Evangelization* (Our Sunday Visitor: 1-800-348-2440).

Pope John Paul II, *The Mission of the Redeemer*, and Pope Paul VI, *Evangelization in the Modern World* (Paulist National Catholic Evangelization Association: 1-800-237-5515).

21   The Dynamics of Fellowship

Participation in small Christian communities provides us support that is essential for Christian living.

He who does not love his brother whom he has seen, cannot love God whom he has not seen. And this commandment we have from him, that he who loves God should love his brother also. 1 John 4:20-21

From the start the Church has drawn great strength from small communities. The earliest churches that launched the Christian movement were small assemblies of neighbors who met in the biggest local house. Over the centuries small groups continued to make the Church dynamic — from the monastic communities in the North African desert, to the brotherhoods and sisterhoods of St. Francis, to the myriad of small communities that enliven the Church today.

The local body of Christ is the source of our Christian lives, and in that assembly, the Lord nourishes and strengthens us through the sacraments. But our parishes are often so huge that the body of Christ remains a nameless collection of individuals. We don't know the other members, so we can't begin to love them.

Small communities help us take the body of Christ seriously, allowing sisters and brothers to get to know and care about each other. They provide us real-life opportunities to obey the Lord's love commandment and to give each other the personal support living as a Christian requires.

Most small Christian communities are built around regular meetings. These gatherings usually include elements like worship, study, personal sharing, and social time. Groups often form around a Christian-action purpose like social justice, evangelization, Catholic family support, and the like. All evoke some degree of personal commitment from members.

Participants in small communities experience numerous benefits, all of which strengthen them and help them tap the power of the sacraments for Christian living. Among these benefits are:

Christian relationships. Participation in Christian communities forges committed friendships among members. My wife and I, for example, have enjoyed lifelong relationships we formed with several couples in Catholic family groups we belonged to thirty years ago.

Personal support. Group members express their love for each other concretely. They often pitch in to help each other when there is a need or a crisis. For example, once when I bought a handyman's dream house, a member of our Catholic family group replumbed the building with me as his assistant. Group members also support each other emotionally and spiritually with encouragements, corrections, and prayers.

Practical wisdom. None of us knows all we need to about Christian living, but regularly talking about it with others lets us pool our wisdom. Participating in a family group, for example, taught my wife and me how to build a Catholic family culture and how to celebrate the sacraments at home.

Accountability. In some groups members make themselves accountable to each other for their spiritual growth. Participants in cursillo groups, for example, share each week about their prayer, study, Christian action, and other areas. Accountability strengthens mutual love and helps ensure our progress in Christian living. For example, once every week for a year I reviewed my time commitments with a friend so he could check me from diverting attention from my wife and children to work, service, and meetings.

Christian environment. Groups generate a social environment that supports the Christian way of life. Christian family groups, for example, have always given our children friends who were following the same patterns they were. Parents in our family groups shared the same ideals, had similar family customs, and insisted on boundaries like ours, so our children had plenty of friends to support their living the way we wanted them to.

The fellowship that small communities offer is not an extra-added attraction, like a free dessert that a restaurant advertises as a come-on. It is the meal itself, an essential for Christian living.

❦

We urge you to join with other couples and families who are making a conscious effort to follow Christ's way of love.

U.S. Catholic Bishops

For Discussion

• How do small groups help us live as Christians?

For Reflection

• How have I benefited from the support of other Christians?
• Where do I find support for my Christian life? Do I participate in a small Christian community?

Application Ideas

• Consider participating in a small Christian community. Find one that seems to match your concerns and needs. If you feel it's necessary, decide to participate for a trial period before joining in a more committed way.
• Parents especially should look for ways to link up with a Catholic family support group. Many parishes sponsor parents groups, and national and international organizations like the Christian Family Movement and Couples for Christ have local chapters. If you don't find anything that suits you, perhaps you should convene a group of your own. A pattern for a parents' group meeting appears on p. 194.

Resources

Numerous organizations support families by forming small, local communities. Among them are: The Christian Family Movement, Couples for Christ, Marriage Encounter, New Families Movement, and Teams of Our Lady. For information about these groups in your area, call your diocesan family life office.

Thomas A. Kleissler, Margo A. Lebert, and Mary C. McGuinness, *Small Christian Communities* (Paulist National Catholic Evangelization Association: 1-800-237-5515).

Baptism

" *The sign of the cross shall appear in the heavens,*
when our Lord shall come to judge the world,
and the servants of the cross,
who conformed themselves here in this life to Christ crucified on the cross,
shall go to Christ their judge
with great faith and trust in him. "

The Imitation of Christ

22  Plunged Into Life

We go down into the waters of baptism to die with Christ, and we rise with him from its waters to live a new life.

We were buried therefore with him by baptism into death, so that as Christ was raised from the dead by the glory of the Father, we too might walk in newness of life. Romans 6:4

Once at a noon Mass in our parish, I witnessed the baptism of a dozen children, ages eight to thirteen. Since it's not every Sunday that a gang of kids gets baptized, I was impressed. Garbed in a brown robe, each child crouched down into a pool of water near the altar. Father doused each with a pitcher full of water. Each rose to be wrapped in a white garment. The congregation burst into loud applause to greet these kids who had just been plunged into God's life.

This striking event illustrated for me the reality of baptism. In baptism we die with Christ and we rise with him to live a new life. When these children went down into the pool, they were entering into Christ's death. Their action signified that they were going with him into his tomb. When they came up from the water, they were rising with Christ. Their emerging from the pool clothed in white robes was a sign of their emerging with Christ from his tomb. Their immersion in water indicated that the children had been plunged into the Holy Spirit, the source of the supernatural life they were now living.

But this event was not just a dramatization of Good Friday and Easter Sunday. We were not pretending that these children were dying and rising with Christ. They were sharing sacramentally in Christ's death and resurrection, which are no less real in baptism than they were on Good Friday afternoon and Easter morning.

Make no mistake about it: Paul's description of baptism in Romans 6:4 was no mere metaphor but a declaration of fact. "We were buried therefore with him by baptism into death, so that as Christ was raised from the dead by the glory of the Father, we too might walk in newness of life." What the Lord portrays to our senses in baptism, he accomplishes in our spirits. So in the sacrament of baptism, Christ's death and resurrection become our death and resurrection.

The water of baptism has another significance. Water cleanses, and everyday we use it for that purpose. For example, we bathe in water. When Father doused that gang of kids with pitchers full of water, he was cleansing their bodies. They were taking baths. All the pouring and splashing was a sign of what was happening in their souls. By the water of baptism, the Lord was cleansing them of sin. The natural signs of cleansing that we observed and that the children felt on their bodies produced a supernatural cleansing for them. Again, this is not a metaphor — baptism is not *like* a bath. It *is* a bath that cleans us up spiritually for our new lives.

As was the case with these children, baptism normally occurs at Mass in the presence of the community. There's a good reason for this. Baptism is the rite of initiation into the Church. It incorporates new members into the body of Christ. The Lord does not give us new life privately as a personal gift. He gives us supernatural life by joining us to a community that is already living it.

The Church also celebrates baptisms during Mass for the benefit of the community. The ceremony catches our attention, reminding us of our own baptism that plunged us into life with Christ.

❦

Some argue against the baptism of infants on the grounds that religion should not be imposed on a child. . . . But baptism does not impose anything; one baptized in infancy still has to take a personal stand for or against Christ when he comes of age. Baptism gives him a grace to help him make the right choice.

Edward D. O'Connor, C.S.C.

For Discussion
• What are the signs of baptism? What do they signify? Why do we celebrate baptisms during Mass?

For Reflection
• What difference has being baptized made in my life?
• Do all family members know what happens in baptism? How can we increase their understanding and awareness?

- Are all family members baptized? If not, what steps can be taken to make it happen?

Application Ideas

- Churches place holy water fonts at every entrance to remind us of our baptism. We take water and sign ourselves with the cross when we come into the assembly. This action should remind us of the new life we share with the other members of the body of Christ. We take water and bless ourselves as we leave the assembly. This is a reminder that we are called to share our new life with others.
- Renew your practice of signing yourself with holy water when you enter and leave church. Use the action to increase your awareness of your life in Christ.
- Teach family members about the significance of this practice. Encourage them to think about their baptism and their new life in Christ when they sign themselves.

Resources

Catechism of the Catholic Church, nos. 1214-1245.
Edward D. O'Connor, *The Catholic Vision* (Our Sunday Visitor: 1-800-348-2440), 393-396.

23 Baptism Is Big News

Celebrating a baptism can be a learning experience and an occasion of grace for all family members.

Blessed be the God and Father of our Lord Jesus Christ. By his great mercy we have been born anew to a living hope through the resurrection of Jesus Christ from the dead. 1 Peter 1:3

Had you flipped on the television news at 11 p.m. on September 12, 1982, you would have learned that forty-four people had been killed in a U.S. helicopter crash in West Germany, that the Chinese Communists had ousted Mao Tse Tung's handpicked successor from his post, that a tropical storm hit Texas, that Chris Evert Lloyd had won her sixth U.S. Open, and that Miss California had been chosen Miss America.

But there would have been no report on the biggest news of that day — the baptism of Mary Catherine Ghezzi, my youngest daughter. Beside it, all the other events of September 12, 1982, pale in significance.

All the news reports that day concerned institutions made by human beings that will pass away in a short time. But the big, untold story was about an immortal, one of God's durable creatures who will live forever. And the news about my little immortal was very big: God had adopted Mary Catherine Ghezzi, begetting her as his own daughter through the Holy Spirit. Forever, from that momentous day on, my child would be superhuman — living a divine life with supernatural privileges.

Since baptisms are such significant events, families should make a big deal of them. We should do everything we can to make them memorable.

When there is to be a baptism in the family, we should involve everyone in preparing for it. Making some contribution to the celebration can be a learning experience and an occasion of grace for all family members. Here are some suggestions:

- Have the family pray together daily for the one who is to be baptized. If the family is expecting a baby, start family prayer for the child as early as possible in the pregnancy. Pray for the little one's healthy physical development and for the Holy Spirit to bring him or her safely to new life in baptism. If the candidate is a child or adult, pray with them regularly as the parish community leads them step by step to baptism.

- Look for chances to have informal conversations with children about what baptism will mean for their baby sister or brother. With older children, study what happens in baptism. Use one of the books recommended in the bibliography.

- On the day of the big event, have a baptism party for the family, godparents, close relatives, and friends. Let all the children help with plans and preparations.

- Do everything possible to create memories of the baptism. Take photographs or videos before and after the baptism. Make a photo album. Save the candle and white robe that the candidate receives. Preserve the front page of the newspaper of the baptism day.

We celebrate birthdays as anniversaries of the start of our children's human lives. We should expand our celebrations to remember the start of their divine lives. We should include remembrances of baptism in birthday celebrations. At birthday parties, light the child's baptismal candle or a candle that stands for it. Display the white robe if you have it, look at photographs of the baptism, show the video. When the child is old enough, show her or him the front page of the newspaper from the baptism day. Explain that the most important news that day was really his or her baptism, and why.

If the family does not expect any more baptisms, look for other ways to make a big deal of the sacrament. Here are some things you could do:

- Study the rite of baptism as a family. Discuss the meaning of different parts of the ceremony and their significance for Christian living.

- Volunteer to work for a year with your parish Rite of Christian Initiation for Adults (RCIA) program. As you learn about the steps adult candidates for baptism will be taking, discuss them with your family. During the year, attend the Masses where the steps occur.

- Find out when your parish will celebrate the renewal of baptismal vows. It usually occurs at the Easter Vigil or on Easter Sunday, but it may be done at other times. Review the renewal of vows with family members beforehand to prepare everyone to make this important commitment.

A Christian is an Alleluia from head to foot.

St. Augustine

For Discussion

- Why can it be said that baptism is more important than any other human event?

For Reflection

- What difference has being baptized made in my life? What would my life be like if I had not been baptized?
- Does everyone in my family appreciate the importance of his or her baptism? What can we do in our family to call attention to the significance of baptism?

Application Ideas

- Consider celebrating your children's baptisms as a part of the family's birthday parties. Create customs that fit the age and personality of each child.

Resources

Catechism of the Catholic Church, nos. 1246-1261.

Peg Bowman, *At Home with the Sacraments: Baptism* (Twenty-Third Publications: 1-800-321-0441).

Robert Hamma, *Together at Baptism* (Ave Maria Press: 1-800-282-1865).

The Rite of Baptism (The Liturgical Press: 1-800-858-5450).

24 Applying the Power of the Cross

 *We should make the sign of the cross often because it opens us to God's action in our daily routines.*

But far be it from me to glory except in the cross of our Lord Jesus Christ, by which the world has been crucified to me, and I to the world. Galatians 6:14

Teaching each of my children to make the sign of the cross has been very rewarding. Somehow it united me with the millions of parents who through the ages taught their little ones this important act. The gestures and the words tell why Catholics make the sign of the cross. Forming the cross over our upper body recalls the horrible instrument on which Jesus overcame sin, death, and Satan for us. The words connect the cross and the life of the Trinity as a reminder of baptism.

The practice stems from baptismal rites in the early Church. Today the celebrant still traces a cross on the foreheads of candidates to mark their initiation into the New Covenant. This action parallels the rite of circumcision that signified incorporation into the Old Covenant. Signing ourselves applies the graces of baptism to our daily lives.

The early Christians encouraged one another to make the sign of the cross as a testimony to their faith in Christ. For centuries Catholic and Orthodox Christians have continued to sign themselves. The gesture has taken different forms. Sometimes a small cross was made with fingers and thumb on the forehead or breast, as we now do at the announcement of the gospel at mass. Christians began to use the larger gesture in the fourth century.

The Greek word that early Christians used for the sign of the cross was the same word used for the mark people put on their possessions. As signs of ownership shepherds marked their sheep, generals tattooed the hands of their soldiers, and the wealthy branded their slaves. Similarly, by signing themselves with the cross, Christians declare that they belong to Christ. Whoever wishes, Jesus said, to "come after me, let him deny himself and take up his cross and follow me" (Mark 8:34). Making the sign of the cross affirms our denial that we belong to ourselves. It declares to the Lord, to ourselves, and to everyone else who it is that owns our lives.

The sign of the cross also invokes spiritual protection for us and our children. The cross, the instrument of Christ's death, was also the instrument of his conquest of Satan, our ancient enemy. Signing ourselves with the cross is a protection because it acknowledges Christ's victory and authority over the evil one and drives him away — cowering.

The Church uses the sign of the cross to confer blessings in the liturgy and encourages us to use it for blessings in daily life. Parents should make the sign of the cross over their children when they pray for them. Signing their foreheads and invoking the Father, Son, and Holy Spirit calls upon the grace of their baptisms to strengthen and defend them. We should sign our boys and girls so that they may be protected from evil influences in their world and from the subtle attacks of the devil.

❧

Let us not be ashamed to confess the Crucified. Let us make the sign of the cross with assurance on our foreheads with our fingers, and so do in all circumstances: when we eat and when we drink, when we come in and when we go out, before we sleep, when we lie down and when we arise.

St. Cyril of Jerusalem

For Discussion

• Why do Catholics make the sign of the cross?
• What does making the sign of the cross say about our relationship to Christ? To the Church?

For Reflection

• What do I think about when I make the sign of the cross? How do I benefit from making it?
• Do all family members know how to make the sign of the cross? Do we sign ourselves with the cross frequently and reverently?

Application Ideas

- Teach family members how to make the sign of the cross. Explain the value it has for Christian living. Begin to use the sign of the cross to open and close all family prayers.
- Start the practice of blessing each other with the sign of the cross. Ask the Lord's blessing in your own words or use formal prayers like the following:

    May the Lord bless us ✠, and preserve us from all evil, and bring us to life everlasting. Amen.

- Pray the sorrowful mysteries of the rosary to help the family discover the power of the cross.
    1. The Agony of Jesus in the Garden of Gethsemane
       Reflect on Mark 14:35-36
    2. The Scourging of Jesus at the Pillar
       Reflect on Mark 15:15
    3. The Crowning of Jesus With Thorns
       Reflect on John 19:2-3
    4. Jesus Walks the Way of the Cross
       Reflect on John 19:16-17; Luke 23:32
    5. Jesus is Crucified and Dies on the Cross
       Reflect on Luke 23:44-46

Resources

Catechism of the Catholic Church, nos. 1262-1270.

Catholic Household Blessings by the National Conference of Catholic Bishops (St. Paul Books & Media: 1-800-876-4463).

25 Godparents — Guides for the Journey

❦ *Sponsoring a person for baptism involves a commitment to disciple them in Christian living.*

Be imitators of me, as I am of Christ. 1 Corinthians 11:1

I had a lot of help along the way to making an adult Christian commitment. A community of friends at college enfolded me in loving relationships and impelled me to embrace their high ideals. But the biggest source of encouragement and strength came from finding a mentor who served me as a guide for my journey. During my sophomore year, I formed a friendship with a professor who became my exemplar. Among many things, he taught me about prayer, the liturgy, the body of Christ, and personal relationship with the Lord. In short, he led me to Christ and discipled me in the faith. He was in a true sense my "godfather."

Jesus arranged that the Christian faith would be handed on from person to person, so godparents have always played a significant role in incorporating newcomers into the Church. In the early Church, they were sponsors who guaranteed that candidates for baptism were genuinely converted to Christ and properly prepared for the sacrament. Over the centuries the role of godparents has evolved, so that now they are responsible for supporting the Christian formation of the one being baptized.

The baptismal liturgy clearly defines the duties of godparents. The celebrant first ensures that the parents agree to raise their child to practice the faith and to love God and neighbor. Then he turns to the godparents and asks, "Are you ready to help these parents in their duty as Christian mothers and fathers?" By saying "We agree," the godparents make a significant commitment to play a role in discipling the child as he or she grows up in Christ.

Today godparenting seems to be a shadow of the reality it is supposed to be. Parents often choose godparents for the wrong reasons — for example, to honor a relative — and people agree to become godparents without much awareness of their duties. If we take the discipleship of our children seriously, then we ought to see to it that we choose godparents who will really support our efforts. Both parents and potential godparents must understand the seriousness of the commitment and the importance of the task.

To perform their duties, godparents should fulfill a number of roles to guide the young person on his or her journey of faith. Godparents should be:

- Exemplars who show the child what it means to practice the Catholic faith and obey the law of love.
- Mentors who instruct the child in the faith and encourage him or her in Christian living.
- Counselors the child trusts enough to go to for advice.
- Intercessors who pray regularly for the child's growth in Christ and journey to final happiness with the Lord.

Before we invite someone to be a godparent, we should determine that the person has the faith commitment to undertake these roles and that no moral or personal problems stand in the way. Godparents should be sure that they have the time and inclination to participate in discipling the child.

To get a godparent in position to influence the child, parents will have to take some deliberate actions. If possible, we should choose godparents who live nearby and perhaps are members of our parish. We should include them in family activities to create chances for them to become friends with the child. For the same reason, we should encourage them to engage in activities with the child one-on-one. Of course, godparents should also take the initiative in showing concern for the child.

Godparents are like gardeners who work hard to foster the life of a plant and are delighted when it produces healthy, delicious fruit. In their case, however, they are fostering supernatural lives that bear fruit that will last forever.

The glory of God is a human person fully alive and the life of such a person consists in beholding God.

St. Irenaeus of Lyons

For Discussion

• What do godparents agree to do for the person they sponsor at baptism?
• In what ways can godparents fulfill their responsibilities?

For Reflection

• In what ways have mentors helped me on my faith journey?
• If you are a godparent, do you pray for the person you sponsored? Are you developing a relationship with the person so that you can encourage and instruct him or her?
• How do the godparents of your children relate to them and to the family? Have you discussed their supportive and discipling role with them? What could you do differently to help them support your children in their faith journeys?

Application Ideas

• Have a conversation with your spouse about godparenting. Agree that, when you have infants or other family members to be baptized, you will take a careful approach to selecting godparents.
• When the time comes to choose godparents for family members, be sure that they understand the seriousness of the commitment and the role.
    - Ask the Holy Spirit to guide you to the right person for your child. Don't invite someone for the wrong reason. Select a person who can support you and influence the child positively.
    - Before inviting the sponsor, have a serious conversation with him or her about the commitment and role of godparents.
• Consider the relationships that exist between godparents and your children. Determine whether the godparents are practicing Catholics who can have a good influence on your children. If so, take steps to help them fulfill their godparenting role.

Resources

Henry Libersat, *Godparents: A Practical Guide for Parents and Godparents* (Servant Publications: 1-800-458-8505).

Confirmation

“ *Heavenly King,*
Consoler,
Spirit of truth,
present in all places and filling all
things,
treasury of blessings and giver of life:
come and dwell in us,
cleanse us of every stain
and save our souls, ”
O gracious Lord.

Byzantine Liturgy

26 Strengthened for Living

🌣 *Confirmation does not end our Christian journey but begins it and equips us to reach the goal of maturity in Christ.*

I bow my knees before the Father . . . that according to the riches of his glory he many grant you to be strengthened with might through his Spirit in the inner man. Ephesians 3:14, 16

Many Catholic parents mistakenly regard the sacrament of confirmation as a graduation. With sighs of relief, they feel that formal religious education for their son or daughter is over. No more nagging him about religion classes, no more dragging her to church on Wednesday nights or Saturday mornings. The job is done — the kid has become an adult Catholic and is on his or her own. If parents think this way, their kids will too, and their confirmation will be a dead end instead of a fresh start.

With baptism and the Eucharist, confirmation is a sacrament of initiation. Confirmation completes the work of baptism, and so is only the end of the beginning of our Christian lives, not the beginning of the end. We can regard the sacrament as a graduation only if we see a graduation as the starting point of our applying education to life. Confirmation does not produce finished adult Catholics. It launches Catholics on the road to Christian maturity and equips them with resources to help them reach it.

The waters of baptism cleanse us, plunge us into God's life and incorporate us into the body of Christ. The signs of confirmation — the laying on of hands and anointing with the oil of chrism — signify that it equips us for our service as Christians.

In its secular roots, laying on of hands indicated the conferral of an office or responsibility on someone. It strengthened a person who was faced with new duties or was entering a new state of life. The laying on of hands signifies our commissioning as disciples charged with continuing Christ's ministry. It "confirms" us in our role as witnesses to Christ.

In biblical times, ointments and oil were commonly used in treating illness and wounds and in the massage of athletes. The anointing of confirmation signifies health and strength and produces supernatural health and strength in the life of the recipient. It enhances our ability to overcome the obstacles we meet along the way to full maturity in Christ.

Baptism and confirmation provide a double dose of the Holy Spirit. In baptism the Lord gives us the Holy Spirit to make us children of God. In confirmation he pours out a fresh gift of the Spirit, who acts as guide and protector for our Christian lives.

The day after we're confirmed, we may not feel much stronger as Christians than we were the day before. But confirmation, like all the sacraments, causes what it signifies and its supernatural effects do not depend on our feelings. The Holy Spirit really makes us stronger. He strengthens us:

- In our relationship to God. Among his gifts are knowledge, fear of the Lord, and piety which increase our intimacy with God, fill us with awe at his majesty, and enflame our hearts with devotion. (See Isaiah 11:2-5.)
- In our relationships with sisters and brothers. "God's love," says Paul, "has been poured into our hearts through the Holy Spirit who has been given to us" (Romans 5:5). That's the love that makes it possible for us to love others unconditionally.
- In our relationships with society. When Jesus commissioned us as disciples to proclaim the gospel to the nations, he promised to give us the Holy Spirit as a source of strength: "And behold, I send the promise of my Father upon you" (Luke 24:49).

Confirmation does not make the Christian life any easier. But it does give us a Companion for the journey, a mighty one who clears the road of debris, points the way out of confusion, and protects us from untold dangers.

❧

All powerful God, Father of our Lord Jesus Christ, by water and the Holy Spirit you freed these candidates from sin. Send your Holy Spirit upon them to be their Helper and Guide.

Rite of Confirmation

For Discussion

• In what sense does confirmation make us adult Christians? What are the signs of confirmation and what do they do? How can we expect the Holy Spirit to strengthen us?

For Reflection

• How have I experienced the Holy Spirit strengthening me?

Application Ideas

• Confirmation gives us the grace to bear witness to what the Lord has done for us, but we often have the hardest time talking to family members about our relationship with God. Speaking about our experience of Christ in the sacraments is an excellent chance to break the silence. Here is a suggestion:
  - Mom, Dad, and anyone else who is confirmed should take some time to reflect on their relationship with God and on how the Holy Spirit has strengthened them.
  - At a series of meals or family prayer times, have one person talk about his or her relationship with the Lord and what the Spirit has done for him or her.
  - At these times, encourage everyone to ask questions or to share examples from their own lives.
  - Close with a prayer to the Holy Spirit.

Resources

Catechism of the Catholic Church, nos. 1285-1296.
Edward D. O'Connor, *The Catholic Vision* (Our Sunday Visitor: 1 800-348-2440), 396-398.

27 Confirmation: A Time for Family Renewal

❦ *The Holy Spirit comes like a waterfall, so when a family prepares a child for confirmation, it can expect to get wet.*

I will pour out my Spirit on all flesh. Joel 2:28

Helping a young man or young woman prepare to receive confirmation should be a family activity. Like all the sacraments, confirmation is an action of the body of Christ, and our little family cell has the significant responsibility to support the member who is approaching it. Preparing a child for confirmation is a chance for Mom, Dad, sisters, and brothers to show their love for the one who is drawing near such an important milestone on his or her Christian journey.

It is also an opportunity for the whole family to experience spiritual renewal. The Holy Spirit usually comes not like a narrowly-targeted laser beam but like a splashing waterfall, drenching everyone who is near. So as your family supports the candidate for confirmation, it can expect to get wet.

In the months leading up to the big event, the family should be talking, studying, and praying with the child to be confirmed. Here are some suggestions:

- At family prayer times, pray informal prayers and the "Come Holy Spirit" for the person to be confirmed and for the whole family.
- Use the parish preparation program as a basis for family conversations and discussions. Gather the family for a short period each week to review what the candidate is studying. Have the child sum up what he or she learned. Use the child's book as a resource for discussion.

Some parishes involve parents in a preparation program, which we should see as an opportunity rather than as an obligation. The more we learn about the sacrament and the Holy Spirit, the more we can teach our children.

- Develop your own home study about confirmation and the Holy Spirit. Decide together on a regular time each week to have family conversations.
- Study together what happens in the rite of confirmation. The main parts of the service are the renewal of baptismal vows; the laying on of hands, whereby the bishop prays for the Holy Spirit to come upon the group as Helper and Guide; and the bishop's anointing of each candidate on the forehead with the oil of chrism with the words, "Be sealed with the Gift of the Holy Spirit."
- Read to the family and discuss Bible stories or other Scripture passages about the Holy Spirit.
- Some parishes encourage candidates to take a new saint's name as a sign of renewing their commitment to God, but others suggest that they simply use their baptismal names. If your child does not have a saint's name, her or she may want to choose one. Help the child to learn about his or her namesake. Have the child tell the family about the saint.
- In confirmation the Holy Spirit equips us to use our gifts in service of God's people. Have a family celebration before the administration of the sacrament in which all family members tell the candidate what gifts he or she has. Take the occasion to let the child know how much he or she is loved. Cap off this sharing with a nice dessert or a trip to an ice cream parlor.
- If possible, include the child's sponsor in these family preparations for the sacrament.

❧

Baptismal Vows

Do you reject sin, so as to live in the freedom of God's children?
Response: I do.

Do you reject the glamor of evil, and refuse to be mastered by sin?
Response: I do.

Do you reject Satan, father of sin and prince of darkness?
Response: I do.

Do you believe in God, the Father almighty, creator of heaven and earth?

Response: I do.

Do you believe in Jesus Christ, his only Son, our Lord, who was born of the Virgin Mary, was crucified, died and was buried, rose from the dead, and is now seated at the right hand of the Father?

Response: I do.

Do you believe in the Holy Spirit, the holy catholic Church, the communion of saints, the forgiveness of sins, the resurrection of the body and life everlasting?

Response: I do.

This is our faith. This is the faith of the Church. We are proud to profess it, in Christ Jesus our Lord. Amen.

Baptismal Rite

For Discussion

• Why should preparing a child for confirmation be a family activity?

For Reflection

• In what ways can our family support the child who is to be confirmed?

Application Ideas

• As preparation for the sacrament, study together the renewal of baptismal vows. Be sure everyone has a basic understanding of the questions and of the importance of affirming them. Encourage everyone to make a heartfelt renewal of their baptismal vows during the confirmation ceremony.

Resources

Catechism of the Catholic Church, nos. 1297-1314.

Peg Bowman, *At Home with the Sacraments: Confirmation* (Twenty-Third Publications: 1-800-321-0411).

The Rite of Confirmation (The Liturgical Press: 1-800-858-4450).

28 Producing the Fruit of the Spirit

The graces of baptism and confirmation are at work, leading us in behaviors that make us more like Christ.

The fruit of the Spirit is love, joy, peace, patience, kindness, goodness, faithfulness, gentleness, self-control. Galatians 5:22-23

No one has to remind us that even though we became sons and daughters of God at baptism, often we don't look very much like our Father. Sin clouds the image of God in us, and so we must be continually transformed. The Lord produces the fruit of the Spirit in us to reform us in his likeness. They are dispositions that sharpen the image of God in us and bring it back into focus. The fruit of the Spirit empowers us to conduct ourselves as Jesus did, acting with love, patience, goodness, and self-control.

Acquiring these traits, then, is very important to us. We cannot do anything to produce the fruit of the Spirit for ourselves, because our transformation in Christ is God's work. But we must do everything we can to cooperate with the Lord. Our role in the process is to apply the grace we receive in the sacraments in our daily lives. God works to make us more like Jesus in three ways: 1) the Holy Spirit produces Christ's character in us; 2) we become like Jesus by spending time worshiping him; and 3) the Father trains us by letting us have problems which can be chances for growth.

The main way we grow in the fruit of the Spirit is by the direct action of the Holy Spirit, whom we receive in baptism and confirmation. When Jesus said that rivers of living water would flow from the hearts of those who believe in him, he was speaking about the activity of the Holy Spirit in us (John 7:38).

As water is the source of life and nurturance for plants in a garden, the Holy Spirit is the source of new life for us. His energy brings forth and nurtures the fruit of the Spirit in us. Just as watering the garden brings forth all kinds of beautiful flowers, the life of the Spirit produces in us love, joy, peace, and all the characteristics of Christ.

Our children become like us by being around us, and we become more like Christ just by being in his presence. This is a second way we develop the fruit of the Spirit. Paul says that as we come before the Lord, we are "being changed into his likeness from one degree of glory to another" (2 Corinthians 3:18). So worshiping at Mass and praying before the Blessed Sacrament can be occasions for us to become more like Christ. If we want to grow in the fruit of the Spirit, we will also spend time daily in personal prayer and take opportunities to pray with our families and other Christians.

Facing problems in faith is a third way for us to grow in the fruit of the Spirit. The Lord lets us have problems as chances to become more like him. We can let them take advantage of us, or we can yield them to the Holy Spirit and make the most of them. Jesus said that to make us fruitful, the Father prunes us like branches on a vine. "Every branch that does bear fruit he prunes, that it may bear more fruit" (John 15:2).

Take compassion and forbearance, for example. Jesus' command to love others as he loved us (John 15:12) did not stipulate that we should serve only those people we like. Jesus knew this would not be easy, but he sent the Holy Spirit to help us. I can count on grace to support me in being kind to those unlovely people I meet at work, at school, at church, and in the neighborhood.

We would never have the chance to develop compassion and forbearance apart from our problems in loving others. The same is true for other fruits of the Spirit. Anger opens the way for patience and fear for courage. Without unruly desires and sexual temptations, what need would we have for self-control and chastity? They would be so tame, they'd be worthless.

❧

Each time anyone comes in contact with us, they must become different and better people because of having met us. We must radiate God's love.

Mother Teresa

For Discussion

- What is the purpose of the fruit of the Spirit? How do we acquire the fruit of the Spirit?
- What is the role of the sacraments in producing spiritual fruit in our lives?

For Reflection

- In what situations has the Holy Spirit helped me behave like Jesus would have?

Application Ideas

- Take younger children to church to make a visit to Jesus in the Blessed Sacrament. Explain that he is present in a special way in the consecrated bread that is reserved in the tabernacle. Also explain that we can spend time praying in his presence, and as we do he gives us the grace to love others, to be kind, to be patient, and so on.
- The fruits of the Spirit have much to do with the way we relate to others, and they help us overcome problems we have with people. Ask older children to identify the problems that they are having in their relationships. Suggest that they select one of these and that they pray to the Holy Spirit for help every day for a week. Recommend that they pick a small or medium-size problem to start with. If appropriate, at the end of the week, ask each one to report on what he or she has learned or what has happened in the relationship.

Resources

Catechism of the Catholic Church, nos. 733-736; 1832.
Edward D. O'Connor, *The Catholic Vision* (Our Sunday Visitor: 1-800-348-2440), 330-333.

29 Cultivating the Fruit of the Spirit

❦ *Obedience, resisting temptation, and imitating Christ
engage sacramental graces to help us conform to God's
will.*

**Do not be conformed to this world but be transformed by the
renewal of your mind, that you may prove what is the will of
God, what is good and acceptable and perfect. Romans 12:2**

When we receive the Holy Spirit in baptism and confirmation, he
does not just come and go. He remains in us as our source of divine
life. He makes Christ present in our hearts, he brings us gifts that equip
us to serve, he gives us wisdom and strength for everyday living, and
he produces fruit in us that makes us more like Jesus.

The fruits of the Spirit are character traits that influence us to
conduct ourselves as Jesus would. To acquire the fruits of the Spirit,
we must apply the graces of the Holy Spirit to our lives. We do this
mainly in three ways: by obeying God's commandments, by resisting
temptation, and by imitating Christ.

Obedience. We know we are reproducing the marks of Christ
when our lives conform to God's will. He taught that we would bear
fruit if we obeyed his commandments, especially that we love one
another as he loved us (John 15:8-10).

God's will is not a mystery to us, because he revealed it in
Scripture. There we find both the Ten Commandments and the New
Testament pattern of life. We also find God's will in the practice and
the laws of the Church, which the Holy Spirit has always guided. Just
as Jesus developed his character by obeying his Father perfectly, we
put on Christ's character by obediently doing all God tells us to do.

Resisting temptation. The life of the Spirit in us runs smack into
the inclinations of our flesh, the self-indulgent residue of our fallen
natures. Evil inclinations churn in us like perpetual motion machines
that generate momentum toward sinful behavior. When evil desires are
propelling us, it takes a decisive intervention to stop us.

When we find ourselves wanting to do something bad, we must act decisively before we reach a point of no return. Paul says that those who belong to Christ "have crucified the flesh with its passions and desires" (Galatians 5:24). Refusing to go along with our bad desires is another way of cooperating with the grace that produces the fruits of the Spirit in us.

Imitation of Christ. The efforts we make at spiritual growth ought to be patterned on someone who lived an exemplary Christian life. "Be imitators of me," said Paul, "as I am of Christ" (1 Corinthians 11:1). We can dispose ourselves to acquiring fruit of the Spirit by imitating others who already manifest it in their lives.

It's not easy to find exemplars today when our culture exalts unworthy celebrities as heroes. But that's why the Church has given us the saints, Christian "celebrities" who have shown us how to live our ordinary human lives as Christ would. When we imitate Christ, we don't get imitations; we get the real thing.

Our cooperation with grace is important, but if we try to claim too big a role in producing the fruit of the Spirit, we would be making a mountain out of a mole hill. A gardener can dink around with a spade, pull some weeds, put in some stakes, and so on, as he tends his plants. But all his labor gives no life or growth to them. Our effort accounts about as much for our spiritual growth. This does not mean we should stop trying to be like Christ. It means we must stop trying to do it on our own and let the Holy Spirit work.

❧

We must serve God as he wishes, not as we choose.

St. Teresa of Ávila

For Discussion

• What is our role in producing the fruit of the Holy Spirit in our lives? How do we know what God wants us to do? What does crucifying the flesh have to do with growing in the fruit of the Spirit?

For Reflection

• What can I do to obey God's commandments more closely? What can I do to resist temptations more effectively? Could my family become more like Christ by imitating me?

Application Ideas

• Plant a small garden with your children to teach the principles of spiritual growth. Have them tend to half of the garden by themselves by weeding, fertilizing, and so on. Talk about the activity and make these points:
  - Water makes the plants grow. It makes it possible for them to live and to be strong and to produce fruit and flowers.
  - The Holy Spirit we receive in baptism is the source of Christian life for us. He gives us Christ's life, makes us strong, and produces the fruit of the Spirit in us.
  - The untended part of the garden did not do as well as the tended part because plants need help from us to grow well. The Christian life is like that. We need to pray, study, and serve God and others to grow strong as Christians.
  - We can do a few things to help plants grow, but we can't give them life. We can do some things to grow stronger as Christians, like praying and obeying God's commandments. But the Holy Spirit is the one who makes it possible for us to be like Jesus. He gives us the grace to love others, to be patient and kind, to be forgiving, and so on.

Resources

The Catechism of the Catholic Church, nos. 2006-2016.
William Odell, *How to Talk to Your Children About Confirmation* (Our Sunday Visitor: 1-800-348-2440).

30 <u>Come, Holy Spirit</u>

 *Confident prayer to the Holy Spirit taps the power of baptism and confirmation for daily living.*

Rekindle the gift of God that is within you. 2 Timothy 1:6

One way to tap into the power of the Spirit we received in baptism and confirmation is to pray confidently for him to act in our lives.

Once, for example, some of my friends and I agreed to pray daily for each other, using the long "Come, Holy Spirit" prayer from the Pentecost Mass. That prayer invites the Holy Spirit to fill our hearts, bringing rest, gifts, wisdom, and other consolations. During the year that we prayed this way, many of us were deeply touched by God and experienced a lasting personal renewal.

Daily prayer for the coming of the Holy Spirit has an ancient precedent. After Jesus ascended to his Father, Mary and the disciples prayed together daily for the coming of the Spirit until his dramatic arrival. (See Acts 1:13-2:4.)

I suggest that families agree to pray the traditional "Come, Holy Spirit" daily for each other for specific periods of time. For example, pray it every day for nine days before a baptism, a confirmation, or the feast of Pentecost. Or do it every day during Lent, or if you dare, every day for a year. To heighten our awareness of what the Lord wants for us and to expand our receptivity to his graces, we can reflect on the phrases of this familiar Catholic prayer:

**Come, Holy Spirit, fill the hearts of your faithful,
and enkindle in them the fire of your love.
Send forth your Spirit and they shall be created; and you shall
renew the face of the earth.
Let us pray. O God, who by the light of the Holy Spirit has
instructed the hearts of the faithful, grant that by the same Spirit
we may be truly wise and ever rejoice in his consolation through
Christ our Lord. Amen.**

Come, Holy Spirit. Although the Holy Spirit already lives in us, he can come to us in new and different ways. When we invite him to come afresh, we open ourselves to a greater participation in the divine life we have received. Like Timothy, we can rekindle the gift of God in us.

Fill the hearts of your faithful. Ideals like pleasure, popularity, success, wealth, and power compete for dominance in our hearts. When we ask the Spirit to fill our hearts, we are telling him to crowd out all these competitors. We are also asking him to make the Lord Jesus more present in us so that we may be "filled with all the fullness of God" (Ephesians 3:19).

Enkindle in them the fire of your love. Here we are asking the Spirit both for a greater experience of God's love for us and an increase of our love for God and his people.

Send forth your Spirit and they shall be created. Even though baptism makes us new creations in Christ, we still need to be renewed in the image of God (Colossians 3:10). The Spirit makes us more like Christ by degrees (2 Corinthians 3:18).

And you shall renew the face of the earth. As the Spirit makes us more like Christ, he equips us to bring aid and comfort to people in need and knowledge of God to people who have not met him. This prayer sends us forth to attend to the needs of others. When we pray it, we should be looking for ways to renew our corner of the face of the earth.

Grant that by the same Holy Spirit we may be truly wise. We have our way of looking at things, and God has his way which is far above ours (Isaiah 55:8). When we pray for true wisdom, we are asking the Spirit to let us see things with God's eyes and to bring our views into line with his.

And ever rejoice in his consolation. The Holy Spirit consoles us by making us aware of the Lord's presence. He brings us rest when we're weary, peace when we're anxious, relief when we're tempted, and comfort when we're distressed.

When we pray this prayer to the Holy Spirit, we're asking for a lot, but not more than he is eager and willing to give. So when we pray to the Spirit and expect him to act, he will do more for us than we can even imagine.

In every human being there is an abyss that only God can fill.

Blaise Pascal

For Discussion

- Why do you think we can expect the Holy Spirit to take an active interest in us? What are we asking the Holy Spirit to do in the phrase, "fill the hearts of the faithful?" In what sense do you think the Holy Spirit "renews the face of the earth?"

For Reflection

- In what area of my life do I have the biggest need? What should I ask the Holy Spirit to do about it?

Application Ideas

- Teach everyone in the family to pray the "Come, Holy Spirit." Make copies for each family member. Encourage all to memorize it. Review the meaning of each phrase so that family members will be able to mean the words when they pray them.
- Agree on a specific period of time to say the prayer daily for each other. Start with a short period, possibly a week or nine days at the most.
- Have a family conversation at the end of the period. Ask people to reflect on their lives during that time to see what the Holy Spirit has been doing in them.

Resources

The Catechism of the Catholic Church, nos. 2562-2565; 2670-2672.
John J. Boucher, *Is Talking to God a Long Distance Call?* (Servant Publications: 1-800-458-8505).

The Eucharist

> *Hail our Savior's glorious Body,*
> *Which his Virgin Mother bore;*
> *Hail the Blood which, shed for sinners,*
> *Did a broken world restore;*
> *Hail the sacrament most holy,*
> *Flesh and Blood of Christ adore!*
> *Come, adore this wondrous presence;*
> *Bow to Christ, the source of grace!*
> *Here is kept the ancient promise*
> *Of God's earthly dwelling place!*
> *Sight is blind before God's glory,*
> *Faith alone may see his face!*

Pange Lingua Gloriosi

31 Offering Ourselves to God

Parallels with ancient forms of worship help us give ourselves more fully to God in the Eucharist.

By the mercies of God . . . present your bodies as a living sacrifice, holy and acceptable to God, which is your spiritual worship. Romans 12:1

Every Sunday morning millions of Catholics all over the world gather around altars to offer sacrifice. *Offer sacrifice.* Sounds a little primitive, doesn't it? I could have said the Catholics gather "to celebrate the liturgy" or "to worship God." But I wanted to jar you a bit, to emphasize that sacrifice is a core activity of the Mass.

The sacrificial element of the Mass has its roots in the culture of the ancient Jews for whom sacrifices were a normal form of worship. Offering sacrifice was also the common practice of many tribal people, and it is one of the ordinary ways humans have always worshiped God. Noticing some significant parallels between the sacrifice of the Mass and sacrifices in ancient cultures will help us appreciate the Eucharist more and celebrate it better. Consider these striking similarities between a parish liturgy and a tribal sacrifice:

- The communities assemble at holy places, the tribe perhaps at a rock on a sacred hill and the parish around an altar in a sanctuary paneled with mahogany.
- In both cases an authorized official, a priest, leads the proceedings. Tribe and parish both see him as a presider that relates them to the one they worship.
- The priest places on the altar victims provided by the communities. He does something to the victims to show that the community no longer possesses the victims; they have been given over to the deity. The ancient priest kills the animal. The celebrant at Mass offers bread and wine so that they become the body and blood of Christ.
- The communities share in a meal, eating part of what was

sacrificed; the ancient people eat some of the roasted meat and the parish consumes the body and blood of Christ.

The actions of the ancient people and the modern parishioners have similar meanings. Both communities are giving gifts to the one they worship. The gifts carry messages to the recipient. They might be: "Lord, forgive us"; "Thank you"; "Spare us"; "Protect us." But there's more to it. In the human activity of gift-giving, the gift stands for the giver. Giving a gift to a friend means that we want to strengthen our relationship with him. Similarly, when human beings offer sacrifice, they are saying, "Lord, here I am. I have put myself in this gift. Take me. Make me one with you."

A communion meal is a common feature of sacrifices. The assembly shares in what was offered to the deity as a sign that he has found the sacrifice acceptable. Our experience of ordinary gift-giving helps explain the point. When we give someone a gift, we look for an indication that the receiver found it acceptable. Sometimes a word of thanks is all that's appropriate, but if the gift is something that can be shared, like candy or fruit, normally the recipient shows acceptance by offering some back to the giver. As the gift stands for the giver, the act of sharing seals the union that the giver was seeking from his friend.

Because Mass is our sacrifice, we should make the most of it by participating deliberately. When the gifts of bread and wine are brought forth from the community, we should be consciously aware that those gifts represent our lives. When the priest raises up the consecrated gifts to the Father, chanting "Through him, with him, in him," we should be pouring out our lives as a "living sacrifice" (Romans 12:1). At the communion meal, we should celebrate our renewed union with God by participating enthusiastically.

❧

Prayer Over the Gifts

Priest: Pray, brethren, that our sacrifice may be acceptable to God, the almighty Father.
People: May the Lord accept the sacrifice at your hands for the praise and glory of his name, for our good, and the good of all his Church.

The Great Amen

Priest: Through him, with him, in him, in the unity of the Holy Spirit, all glory and honor is yours, almighty Father, forever and ever.

People: Amen.

Liturgy of the Eucharist

For Discussion

• What characteristics does Mass have in common with other sacrifices? In what ways is a sacrifice like gift-giving?

For Reflection

• At Mass do I deliberately offer myself to God as part of Jesus' sacrifice? Do I see communion as God's saying that he accepts me and unites me to himself?

Application Ideas

• Have a family discussion about the Mass as a sacrifice. Talk about the prayer and the great amen above. Bring out these points:
  - At Mass we unite ourselves to the gifts of bread and wine.
  - With Christ we offer ourselves to God.
  - At communion God accepts our gift of ourselves and unites us to himself.

• Encourage family members to offer themselves to God at Mass. The prayer over the gifts is an appropriate moment to consciously include ourselves in the gifts and the great amen is our opportunity to offer ourselves with Christ.

Resources

The Catechism of the Catholic Church, nos. 1322-1344.

Bert Ghezzi, *How to Talk to Your Children About the Eucharist* (Our Sunday Visitor: 1-800-348-2440).

32 Our Sacrifice, Our Meal

🐾 *At Mass we offer Christ's sacrifice with him, giving ourselves to God and receiving union with him in return.*

"This is my body which is given for you. Do this in remembrance of me. . . . This cup which is poured out for you is the new covenant in my blood." Luke 22:19-20

For thousands of years the Jewish people offered regular sacrifices that God required in the law of Moses. But while these sacrifices were a fitting worship of God, all the blood of sheep and goats spilled on Israel's altars was not enough to completely close the gap between God and human beings that Adam's sin had opened. Nothing achieved this until Jesus' death on the cross.

Jesus' death on Calvary was a sacrifice. Jesus was the victim. The night before he died, he spoke of his body that would be given for us and his blood that would be shed to found a new covenant between God and humans (Luke 22:19-20). Jesus was also the priest, the one making the offering. He said he had the power to lay down his life and to take it up again (John 10:17-18). In his submission to his executioners, Jesus offered himself in sacrifice.

Jesus' death at Calvary was the perfect sacrifice that restored the relationship between God and his creatures. No further sacrifice would ever be necessary. But while this put an end to the need for the sacrifices of the Mosaic law, it did not put an end to worship of God. Indeed, Jesus' sacrifice opened the way for us to come into God's presence and offer him a better worship than ever before. (See John 4:21-24.)

Jesus did not want to leave us without an expression of worship that suited the kind of beings that we are. He wanted everything in the body of Christ to suit our human nature. Human beings are spirits expressed in bodies. The natural way to communicate with our spirits is through our senses. In order that his actions to sanctify our spirits would fit our human nature, Jesus designed the sacraments as signs involving sound, sight, taste, and touch. Offering sacrifice and sharing a communion meal is a human way to express worship. So Jesus instituted the sacrament of the Eucharist to enable us to offer his perfect sacrifice with him and deepen our union with him.

Jesus' death and resurrection are just as real on our altars as they were historically in Jerusalem, but now they appear under sacramental signs. At Calvary, Jesus offered sacrifice as he then was — in his ρhysical body. But in the Eucharist, Jesus offers sacrifice as he now is — in his whole body, the body of Christ, the Church. Not only do we have the privilege of offering Christ's sacrifice, we also get to offer ourselves united to him as members of his body.

At Mass we offer ourselves to God. We are in the body of Christ that the Lord offers to his Father. When God accepts the gifts, he accepts us and unites us to himself. He acknowledges his acceptance and forges a union with us by inviting us to participate in the communion meal. By consuming the body and blood of Christ, we receive the union with God we sought by offering the sacrifice.

Sharing in the Eucharist is also a continuation of the fellowship meals that Jesus shared with his followers. The Last Supper was not the only supper that Jesus ate with his friends. It was the culmination of many meals that expressed the fellowship between Jesus and his disciples. The Mass continues this dimension of the union between Jesus and his followers. It points our attention toward the final meal that we will enjoy with Jesus in his kingdom, the "supper of the Lamb" (Revelation 19:9).

At the Last Supper . . . our Savior instituted the Eucharistic sacrifice of his body and blood. He did this to perpetuate the sacrifice of the cross throughout the centuries until he should come again, and so to entrust to his beloved spouse, the Church, a memorial of his death and resurrection: a sacrament of love, a sign of unity, a bond of charity, a paschal banquet "in which Christ is consumed, the mind is filled with grace, and a pledge of future glory is given to us."

Vatican Council II
Constitution on the Sacred Liturgy

For Discussion
- In what ways was Jesus' death on the cross a sacrifice?
- Why did Jesus establish a sacrificial meal as our form of worship?
- How does the Eucharist make us more one with God?

For Reflection
- Do I take full advantage of the benefits the Lord offers me in the Eucharist? What could I do differently to draw closer to him in this sacrament?

Application Ideas
- Use a gift-giving situation to teach younger children about offering sacrifice. Arrange for a child to give a sharing gift to a relative or friend. Prepare the recipient so that he or she will respond by inviting the child to share in the gift. Discuss the experience with the child drawing the parallel between gift-giving and offering ourselves to God at Mass.

Resources
Catechism of the Catholic Church, nos. 1345-1381.
Ian Petit, O.S.B., *This Is My Body: A Guide to the Mass* (The Liturgical Press: 1-800-858-5450).

33 Getting the Most out of Mass

 *Before, during, and after Mass, we can take practical steps to give ourselves more fully to God.*

Let the word of Christ dwell in you richly, teach and admonish one another in all wisdom, and sing psalms and hymns and spiritual songs with thankfulness in your hearts to God. Colossians 3:16

When a child makes the inevitable complaint, "I don't get anything out of Mass," parents should be able to ask, "What have you put into it?" So we must take some steps to ensure that the family experiences the benefits of its worship.

Of course we get something out of Mass even with minimal personal involvement. The Lord is there loving the teenager who dozes off during the homily, but the teen may only experience boredom. The sacraments do what they are supposed to do — make present the Lord and his saving grace — even if we are not aware of it or are not taking part in the action. But when we worship actively with awareness and faith, the Lord can accomplish much more in us.

Families can do some things before, during, and after Sunday Mass to help each member put as much as possible into worship so as to get as much as possible out of it.

Before Mass. Parents should prepare their kids for Sunday Mass by helping them understand what it's all about. This preparation involves both long-term and short-term study, instruction, and action. Here are some suggestions:

- Study the Mass together. Use a children's missal, borrow a missalette from church, or choose a good book. Discuss what goes on in each major part of the Mass: the introductory rites, the liturgy of the Word, the liturgy of the Eucharist, communion, and the concluding rite. Parents can be learning right along with the children.
- Select key parts of the liturgy and decide how the family will

use them to stimulate awareness, faith, and active participation. For example, a family might select:

- The penitential rite to repent of the past week's sins.
- The gospel to get the Lord's perspective for next week.
- The creed to express our faith.
- The offertory to place ourselves in Christ's sacrifice.
- The great amen to offer ourselves to God with Christ.
- The communion to receive God's acceptance.
- The dismissal to remind us to live out our worship.

- Consider getting directly involved in the liturgical services. Family members can be lectors, ushers, acolytes, musicians, singers, ministers of the Eucharist, ministers to the sick, and so on.

- Families can make more immediate preparations for a Sunday Mass by reading and discussing the Scriptures beforehand, possibly at family prayer times.

During Mass. Try to find seats that allow a good view of the altar. Mass is a drama that catches us up in the Lord's saving acts, so we want the family to be able to see what's going on. Be sure that everyone has song books to help them participate. Mom and Dad can coach the children, reminding younger ones especially, for example, of the key actions the family may have chosen to focus everyone's attention. Above all, parents must set a good example by actively participating themselves.

After Mass. Look for ways of extending the celebration on Sunday and during the week. Consider these ideas:

- Talk about the gospel and the homily while driving home. With younger children, pick out some simple message that applies to them. With older children, ask everyone to say what struck them most in the reading or homily and to explain why. If you disagree with something in the homily, offer a different perspective without being critical of the homilist.

- Continue the celebration by having a breakfast that the kids like. Consider doing something together as a family on Sunday afternoon.

- At family prayer times during the week, talk about what the family can do differently to apply the message of Sunday's Mass.

All these activities before, during, and after Mass will help families get more out of worship. But beneath everything else, the one thing that will benefit them most is coming to know the Lord as a person who loves them. Communicating that reality to kids is a parent's most important task.

❦

All the religion courses and homilies in the world will remain as cold as calculus unless one has a commitment to the person religion is all about.

William J. O'Malley, S.J.

For Discussion

• Why must we work at actively participating in Sunday worship?

For Reflection

• How does my family prepare for Mass? What could we do differently to prepare ourselves more fully?

Application Ideas

• Review the suggestions above and select one that will both have the biggest effect on your family and be easy to accomplish. Carefully plan what it will take to implement that idea and then do it.

Resources

The Catechism of the Catholic Church, nos. 1382-1401.

Archbishop Daniel E. Pilarczyk, *Understanding the Mass* (Our Sunday Visitor: 1-800-348-2440).

Peter M. J. Stravinskas, *Rubrics of the Mass* (Our Sunday Visitor: 1-800-348-2440).

34 Celebrate Passover at Easter

❦ *Celebrating the Passover meal is an ideal way to prepare our hearts for Easter and to learn the meaning of the Eucharist.*

This day shall be a memorial day for you, and you shall keep it as a feast to the LORD; throughout your generations you shall observe it as an ordinance for ever. Exodus 1-5:14

Twelve hundred years before Christ, God delivered the Israelites from bondage in Egypt. He had commanded each family to sacrifice a lamb and to smear its blood on their door posts. This would signal the angel of death, who was coming to slay all Egypt's firstborn, to pass over their houses. The Israelites were to roast the lamb and eat it with unleavened bread because they were departing hastily and had no time for it to rise.

This sacrificial meal was not to be a one-time event. The Lord commanded the Jews to celebrate it annually in their homes as a memorial. Nor was it to be merely an anniversary, like a fourth of July picnic marking the Declaration of Independence, but a sacred remembrance. From that time, every father was to explain to his son that he commemorated Passover "because of what the Lord did for me when I came out of Egypt" (Exodus 13:8).

The climactic events of Jesus' life coincided with the Passover season. During the celebration of this Jewish feast, the Lord's death and resurrection became the Christian Passover that freed us from the bondage of sin and death.

The night before Jesus offered himself on the cross, he commemorated Passover with his disciples at the Last Supper. During that meal he founded the Eucharist, the sacrificial meal that is the heart of Christian worship. Like Passover, the Last Supper was neither a one-time event nor an anniversary. Jesus gave the Eucharist to us as a memorial that would make his sacrifice present for us until time's end. Thus, the Last Supper was the "first supper" of the New Covenant.

Jesus himself became our Passover Lamb, the perfect victim of the perfect sacrifice. He changed the bread that was broken during the meal into his body that would be broken for us; he changed the wine that was blessed and shared into his blood that would be shed for us, so that we could represent his sacrifice at Mass.

Many Catholic families and parishes include a celebration of the Passover meal as part of their Easter celebrations. Our family has done it regularly and has benefited greatly. The reenactment helps us to understand the Jewish heritage of Christianity and to prepare our hearts for the holy week celebrations. A Passover meal can also serve as a living instruction on the Eucharist and the Mass. We have used it as part of the first communion preparation for our children.

Our Passover celebration is the most elaborate of our family's liturgical customs. It takes work, and we enlist all family members as volunteers. Many hands must cooperate to help prepare all the special foods, for example, chopping the apples and nuts to make the reddish "haroses" that recalls the mortar the Jewish slaves had used on construction in Egypt. We often invite guests who are also encouraged to help by bringing a part of the meal.

Booklets are available to assist families and parishes to celebrate the Passover meal in its contemporary format. We have always explained to our family that the Passover meal foreshadows the Mass, and we have called attention to moments during the meal when the Lord may have founded the Eucharist. We also like to conclude the meal by having everyone read a portion of Jesus' last discourse (John 13-17).

Why not celebrate the Passover meal in your home this year? You can take the opportunity to tell your children that you are celebrating it to commemorate what the Lord did for you and your family when he died on the cross and walked out of the tomb alive.

❦

O Day of Resurrection!
Let us beam with festive joy!
Today indeed is the Lord's own Passover,
For from death to life, from earth to heaven
Christ has led us

As we shout the victory hymn!
Christ has risen from the dead!

St. John of Damascus

For Discussion

• What is the connection between Passover and Easter? Between the Passover meal and the Eucharist?

For Reflection

• How could I and my family benefit from celebrating the Passover meal?

For Application

• At the beginning of the next Lenten season, make plans to hold a celebration of the Passover meal during holy week. Gather the materials you will need well in advance — booklets, recipes, song books and so on.

Resources

"The Passover Celebration" (The Liturgy Training Publications of the Archdiocese of Chicago: 1-800-933-7094).

35 The Climax of the Christian Year

❦ *Holy Thursday, Good Friday, and the Easter Vigil are*
opportunities for personal renewal that we should not
miss.

"Do not be afraid; for I know that you seek Jesus who was
crucified. He is not here; for he has risen, as he said."
Matthew 28:5-6

Our celebration of Christ's life through the year climaxes during the
three days before Easter Sunday. On this holy Thursday, Friday, and
Saturday we commemorate the Lord's death and resurrection, the most
important events in all human history. These are pivotal days because they
mark Jesus' founding of the new covenant that restored our relationship
with God. They remind us that Jesus came as the light dismissing
darkness; as the victor destroying the evil one, sin, and death; and as the
savior, giving us a new life and the hope of a glorious union with God.

Where would each of us be without the events the Church presents
on these days? Lost, wandering in gloom, imprisoned by fear, doomed
to eternal nothingness. Thankfully, none of these apply to us as a result
of the mercies of Christ represented in the liturgies of Holy Thursday,
Good Friday, and the Easter Vigil. Because these three days
commemorate the saving actions of Christ that are of profound personal
importance to each of us, we should celebrate them with the Christian
community. We should not miss these annual opportunities to enter more
fully ourselves into the mystery of Christ's death and resurrection.

Early on Holy Thursday evening, we assemble for the liturgy of the
Lord's Supper. The night before he died, Jesus arranged that his death and
resurrection would always be present for us. He transformed the Passover
meal, which represented the deliverance of Israel from slavery, into the
Eucharist, which represents our deliverance from slavery to sin and death.

This liturgy focuses on God's love for us and the love he expects
us to have for others. It culminates in the Eucharist, but another
memorial of the Last Supper provides a dramatic highlight. After the

gospel account of Jesus' washing the feet of his disciples, the presider washes the feet of representatives of the community, a moving demonstration of Christian love.

According to ancient Christian custom, we do not celebrate the sacraments on Good Friday or Holy Saturday. We gather on Good Friday for a starkly simple celebration of the Lord's Passion in a liturgy of the Word, veneration of the cross, and holy communion. We assemble in silence before the altar, which has been stripped as the Lord was before his crucifixion. We hear readings that present Jesus as the suffering servant and high priest of the new covenant, the human-divine mediator whose perfect sacrifice reestablished our oneness with God.

Then we process through the church to worship the cross individually. With a genuflection and a kiss, we honor the wood of the cross, the tree on which the New Adam hung, to redeem us from the heritage of the first Adam, whose fall was occasioned by a tree. We conclude by receiving communion, an opportunity for us to express sorrow for sin and appreciation for the Lord's unselfish love.

The Easter Vigil, celebrated at nightfall on Holy Saturday, is the summit of the Christian year. With great drama, the event is made sacramentally present and we celebrate the resurrection of Jesus.

- We begin the liturgy in darkness, but the paschal candle dispels the darkness, ushering in the true Light, who overcame not only darkness, but sin, death, and the evil one.
- We reflect on readings that recount the history of our salvation that culminates in the events of this sacred night.
- We participate in all the sacraments of initiation. We celebrate baptism and confirmation with catechumens who have prepared for a year to enter into the mysteries we remember most of all at this service — our participation in the Lord's death and resurrection and our strengthening in his Spirit.
- We stand before the Lord to declare our allegiance to him as his disciples by renewing our own baptismal vows.
- We celebrate the Eucharist, our personal Easter, our resurrection with Jesus to our new lives.

There are some occasions we would not even think of missing. A son's graduation, a daughter's wedding, our own twenty-fifth anniversary party — we would not be absent from such important celebrations. We should approach the Christian celebrations of Holy Thursday, Good Friday, and the Easter Vigil the same way. Every year they are the most important days of our Christian lives.

❧

This is the night when Jesus Christ broke the chains of death and rose triumphant from the grave.
What good would life have been to us, had Christ not come as our Redeemer?
... O happy fault, O necessary sin of Adam, which gained for us so great a Redeemer!

Proclamation from the Easter Vigil

For Discussion

• Why are the events remembered on Holy Thursday, Good Friday, and Holy Saturday central to human history? Why should we participate in their annual celebration?

For Reflection

• How would I benefit from joining in the Holy Thursday, Good Friday, and Easter Vigil celebrations?
• Will there be any obstacles this year to my participation in these liturgies? What can I do to overcome them?

Application Ideas

• Individually or as a family, study the Holy Thursday, Good Friday, and Easter Vigil celebrations.
• Plan to celebrate the liturgies of these important days as a family. If circumstances prevent attending all, choose the Easter Vigil. Create family customs that make these events special for kids. Our family, for example, continued the celebration of the Easter Vigil by treating all to hot fudge brownie sundaes.

Resources

The Catechism of the Catholic Church, nos. 638-655; 992-1004.
James Monti, *The Week of Salvation* (Our Sunday Visitor: 1-800-348-2440).

Matrimony and Holy Orders

" *The gift of the Spirit is a commandment of life for Christian spouses and at the same time a stimulating impulse so that every day they may progress toward an ever richer union with each other on all levels — of the body, of the character, of the heart, of the intelligence and will, of the soul — revealing to the Church and to the world the new communion of love.* "

Pope John Paul II

" *Let everyone revere the deacons as Jesus Christ, the bishop as the image of the Father, and the presbyters as the senate of God and the assembly of the apostles. For without them one cannot speak of the church.* "

St. Ignatius of Antioch

36 Collaborators in Creation

 *Matrimony is a wellspring of grace for couples and allows them to cooperate with God in creating a new life.*

"For this reason a man shall leave his father and mother and be joined to his wife, and the two shall become one." This is a great mystery, and I mean in reference to Christ and the church. Ephesians 5:31-32

Two sacraments make possible the growth of the body of Christ by creating new life. Matrimony brings children into the Christian community, ensuring that its numbers will increase. Holy orders empowers leaders in the Church to initiate and nurture these children in the divine life.

Before marriage became a Christian sacrament, it was already a profoundly important human institution. Because in marriage God arranged that "two become one flesh," couples have a physical way to express their mutual love. The sexual union of husband and wife produces new human lives. This is a process that surpasses merely human powers. Other physical acts produce their results naturally, as eating food results in nourishment. But sexual intercourse cannot generate a new human life without the direct and special act of God in creating a new human soul. Thus marriage makes women and men collaborators in the Lord's continuing work of creation.

There is a resemblance in marriage to the loving relationship that exists among the persons of the Trinity. Scripture says that "God created man in his own image . . . male and female he created them" (Genesis 1:27). Some theologians have seen the mutual love of the First Person and the Second Person as the origin of the Third Person. So in marriage the mutual love of two persons becomes embodied in a third person, their child.

In the sacrament of matrimony, Christ supernaturalized the institution of marriage. The sign of matrimony is the union of husband and wife expressed in the vows they exchange. Husband and wife are the ministers of grace to each other. The priest, with the community, is simply the witness of the sacrament.

After the wedding the marriage continues to be a sign through which Christ makes himself present in the Church. To the degree that the spouses serve and love one another humbly and selflessly, their marriage becomes a living parable that shows other people, including their children, what Christ's love for the Church is like. The mystery of two people becoming so deeply joined together that they are, in a sense, two parts of a larger whole, represents the mystery of Jesus' union with us. So Paul writes that the union of husband and wife reflects the union of Christ and the Church.

For the spouses themselves, the sacrament of matrimony is a wellspring of graces, providing the spiritual resources that they need to build life together. Uniting two lives with conflicting preferences, habits, and expectations is not easy to accomplish and requires plenty of divine assistance. When husbands and wives find it difficult to love each other unselfishly, they can trust that God will give them graces for overcoming the difficulties. Parents can also rely on the sacramental graces to help them through the ordeals they face in preparing their children both for successful lives on earth and for eternal life in heaven.

❧

When a Christian man and woman unite in holy marriage, they dedicate themselves to God for a holy service, the extension of his kingdom among humankind. . . . Christ and the church, his bride, have as their first objective to form a worshiping community to praise the Father. So also a husband and wife.

Godfrey Diekmann, O.S.B.

For Discussion

- In what sense does the creation of new life by the sexual union of husband and wife surpass merely human powers?
- In what practical ways do the graces of matrimony help a husband and wife?

For Reflection

• How has my family benefited from the graces of matrimony?

Application Ideas

• Look for ways to speak to your children about the place of sex in marriage. Our culture is supersaturated with illicit sexuality, and our kids get confusing and amoral messages. Parents should explain to their children that God designed sexual intercourse to have a special place in marriage. There he collaborates with husband and wife to create a new human being. Because sex is so closely tied into God's love and plan for us, it is not something to be toyed or experimented with.

Resources

Catechism of the Catholic Church, nos. 1601-1617.

Pope John Paul II, *On the Family* (*Familiaris Consortio*) (St. Paul Books & Media: 1-800-876-4463).

37 Parent Power

 *Matrimony gives parents a continuing grace that helps them prepare children for their human and eternal lives.*

"I will not leave you desolate. I will come to you." John 14:18

Preparing children for life is a demanding job, possibly the most difficult task any adult faces. For a generation and often more, parents serve their kids and stand with them through good times and bad in order to get them off to a good start. We love them at great personal cost, sacrificing time, energy, money, interests, and more, without expecting a return. But we also love them joyfully because we anticipate the satisfaction of seeing them launched, the parents' equivalent of NASA engineers watching the space shuttle pierce the skies at Cape Canaveral.

Sometimes we make child rearing even harder by trying to accomplish it entirely on our own strength. We are a little like the benighted logger who laboriously used a chain saw to cut trees — without turning on the power. When the switch was flipped on, he was startled, and then delighted, with his powerful helper. We are also like the logger with chain saw turned on when we discover the parent power in the sacrament of matrimony.

The grace of matrimony does not quit on our wedding days. Its source is the Holy Spirit, who remains with us, empowering us for married life. He is our best family Counselor, Teacher, and Helper, and we don't rely on him nearly as much as we ought.

Prayer is our means for tapping the power of matrimony. We should pray daily for God's direction and help in caring for our children. We should always intercede for them in our personal prayer times. But moms and dads should also pray together for their families.

If we have never done it, praying aloud together can be intimidating. There is something very personal about opening our hearts to the Lord in another's presence, and we fear the exposure. But revealing our inmost selves in prayer helps us achieve the intimacy we sought when we married. Praying together for our kids gives us a good reason to start. The side effect may be an adventure in unity we had not expected.

When we pray, we can ask the Holy Spirit to help us in such areas as:

- Expressing affection in what we say and do.
- Putting the care and assistance of other family members ahead of our own preferences.
- Seeking forgiveness for our offenses and freely forgiving others.
- Telling other family members about our experience with the Lord and helping them discover a personal relationship with him.
- Building a Catholic family culture and forming children in the Catholic faith.
- Teaching family members basic Christian living — prayer, study, service, and fellowship.
- Developing and communicating a Catholic moral and social justice perspective.
- Helping the family reach out in service to others.

Prayer engages God's power for family living because our children are also his daughters and sons. He made them his own children by bestowing the Spirit on them in baptism. He cares about their lives even more than we do, and it's his heart's desire to have them with him. So when we ask the Lord to draw our kids to himself, we can expect him to say yes. Because of his love for us and for our children, we can also rely on him to intervene in our everyday concerns.

❦

The gift of Jesus Christ is not exhausted in the actual celebration of the sacrament of marriage, but rather accompanies the married couple throughout their lives.

Pope John Paul II

For Discussion

- What is the grace of matrimony? How can we apply it to our family life?
- Why can we expect God to say yes to our prayers for our children?

For Reflection

• In what ways has the grace of matrimony helped my family? What can I do differently to engage the Holy Spirit's power for family living?

Application Ideas

• Consider starting a parents' prayer time. Here are some suggestions that will help you:
   - Decide to take five or ten minutes once a week to pray together for the family.
   - Agree to do it for at least six weeks; then review and renew your commitment.
   - Pick a time that's always available for both Mom and Dad, maybe one evening just after the kids are bedded down.
   - Find a place to pray where both will be comfortable and where you will not be interrupted.
   - Start with the prayer to the Holy Spirit and close with the Lord's Prayer.

   But in between these formal prayers, take turns speaking simply and directly to the Lord about your children and your family's needs.

   You may also take some time to talk about the spiritual condition of the family. But remember that talking things over is one thing and talking to the Lord about them is another.

Resources

Catechism of the Catholic Church, nos. 1638-1642.

Catholic Parent (bimonthly magazine; Our Sunday Visitor: 1-800-348-2440).

Bert Ghezzi, *Keeping Your Kids Catholic* (Servant Publications: 1-800-458-8505).

Bert Ghezzi, *Guiltless Catholic Parenting from A to Y* (Servant Publications: 1-800-458-8505).

38 Priests — Sustaining the Body of Christ

Holy orders gives priests a share in Christ's mediation so that they can bring life and nourishment to the Church.

His gifts were that some should be . . . pastors and teachers, equipment of the saints, for the work of ministry, for building up the body of Christ. Ephesians 4:11-12

Divine life comes to us through the body of Christ. Christ is the head and we are his members, the Church, the organism through which Christ now continues his work. Members of the body of Christ perform different functions that contribute to its growth and health. For example, the Lord has given us missionaries to evangelize and teachers to communicate wisdom.

Among the life-giving servants the Lord has provided are those who are ordained as bishops, priests, and deacons to carry on the work of pastoring, teaching, and equipping the body of Christ. To say that they are "ordained" is to emphasize that the Church is a body with "order," and that some members are chosen to lead it in an "orderly" way.

There is only one Christian priesthood, which is the priesthood of Christ, and one Christian sacrifice, the sacrifice of Christ. Under the old covenant there were many priests who performed many sacrifices. But none of these were able to bring men and women directly and fully into God's presence. Jesus, however, is the perfect priest of the new covenant whose eternal sacrifice gives us access to God.

The sacrament of holy orders does not create new mediators between God and human beings. It draws those who are ordained into the priesthood of the one mediator. By the laying on of hands and anointing with oil, the signs of this sacrament, Christ's mediation is made present in new servants.

Priests, like all members of the body of Christ, are imperfect and mortal. But working through them is Jesus, the perfect priest. Priests are representatives of Christ. They speak on his behalf. In the sacrament of reconciliation, for example, they do not say, "Christ absolves you," but "I absolve you."

Priests make Christ present by speaking his words, by carrying on Christ's work in the Church. Thus by administering the sacraments of initiation, priests cooperate with Christ in begetting new sons and daughters for God's family. By offering Christ's sacrifice in the Eucharist, priests collaborate with the Lord in providing spiritual food to nourish us. In the sacraments of reconciliation and anointing of the sick, priests tend to the health of the body of Christ.

Note, however, that their leadership is designed to spur the activity of the whole body. The leaders do not act *instead* of the members. They are supposed to equip the members so that all the members can undertake their particular roles of service.

To be the personal representative of the one who obediently offered himself to the Father is a pretty tall order. No one responds to such a call without struggle and failure. But for all their weaknesses, we can be thankful for those among us who do specially share in Christ's priesthood, so that his work of forgiveness and transformation in us might go forward.

❦

It is to the priests that all must have recourse who want to live in Christ, for it is from them that they will receive comfort and spiritual nourishment; from them that they will take the salutary remedy enabling them to rise healed and strengthened from the disaster of sin; from them that they will receive the blessing that sanctifies the life of the home, and the sacrament that speeds the last breath of this mortal life on its way to everlasting happiness.

Pope Pius XII

For Discussion
• What is the role of priests in the body of Christ?
• In what sense is a priest a representative of Christ?

For Reflection
• In what ways have priests helped me live the Christian life?

Application Ideas

- Bishops, priests, and deacons perform a significant and challenging work in the Church. Discuss ways your family might express love and support for the clergy who serve you. Consider these possibilities:
  - Pray for your bishop, priests, and deacons regularly during family prayer.
  - Occasionally invite those who serve in your parish to join your family for a meal or a celebration.
  - Include your clergy in family events like attending sports events or other entertainments.
  - Ask the priests, and deacons what your family could do to serve them.
- The priesthood is a vocation that comes from the Lord. Parents should encourage sons to be open to this possibility. We should be careful not to think, speak, or act in ways that communicate to sons that the priesthood is not for them. Rather, we should show high regard for vocations as opportunities to serve the Lord in a significant way. Here are some ways to encourage young men to consider whether they have a calling to the priesthood:
  - Pray regularly for vocations and for young men, including our own sons, to be open to hearing the Lord's call.
  - Encourage sons to serve as acolytes at Mass.
  - Find ways of developing a family friendship with a priest who can serve as a model of dedication and commitment.
- Plan to attend the next ordination in your diocese. Study the sacrament of holy orders and review the rite of ordination beforehand. Take time before and after the event to talk with your family about the priesthood and the sacrament.

Resources

Catechism of the Catholic Church, nos. 1537-1553.

Edward D. O'Connor, *The Catholic Vision* (Our Sunday Visitor: 1-800-348-2440), 408-411.

Father Kenneth Roberts, *Playboy to Priest* (Our Sunday Visitor: 1-800-348-2440).

Reconciliation and Anointing of the Sick

> " *This is the Lamb of God who takes away the sins of the world. Happy are they who are called to his supper.* "

> " *Lord,*
> *I am not worthy to receive you, but only say the word and I shall be healed.* "

Liturgy of the Eucharist

39 Why Go to Confession?

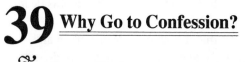 *Reconciliation restores us to spiritual health, but the main reason for using it is that we meet Jesus there.*

For if while we were enemies we were reconciled to God by the death of his Son, much more, now that we are reconciled, shall we be saved by his life. Romans 5:10

Back in the 1940s and 1950s, Catholics went to confession much more frequently than we do now. People like my mother confessed every Saturday in preparation for Sunday Mass. They mistakenly believed that they could never receive communion unless they had recently gone to confession. As a result, on any Sunday, half the congregation might have stayed away from communion.

Now things are reversed. With few exceptions the entire congregation receives communion at Mass. That's an improvement because in the Eucharist the Lord nourishes our spirits and keeps the body of Christ healthy. But in making that change we have also lost something; in recent times, hardly anyone goes to confession at all, let alone frequently.

Today Catholics emphasize the love of God more than we did a generation ago. We celebrate his generous mercy toward us, especially his giving up his Son in death so that we might have life. While we are more focused on the gospel now, in our exaltation of God's love, we tend to minimize our sinfulness, the very reason we need his mercy, Christ's sacrifice, and the gospel. If we were more wary of sin's consequences, no one would have to persuade us to make regular use of the sacrament of reconciliation.

Sin diminishes our sharing in God's life, and in its worst cases, it separates us from him. Sin also damages and even breaks our relationships with others in the body of Christ. Sin is a serious problem because it is bigger than we are. On our own we could not do a thing about it. God recognized our helplessness and intervened to save us.

He sent Jesus to destroy sin in his body on the cross. Thus by his death, the Lord Jesus reconciled us to his Father.

The miracle of our baptism is that it both cleanses us of sin and, through our participation in Christ's death, frees us so that we do not have to sin again. But even though sin's hold on us is broken, we still fall many times each day. Because of our weakness and bad inclinations, we need a continuing means to deal with sin, or it will conquer us again. So Jesus gives us the sacrament of reconciliation as the normal way for us to receive God's forgiveness. Of course, when we sin we can and should ask forgiveness directly of the Lord. A simple prayer of repentance may be enough to take care of our sins, but we should also use the sacrament. That's because sin is not a purely private affair. It affects the whole Christian community. When sin diminishes divine life in one member, the whole body of Christ is weakened. The body uses the sacrament of reconciliation to restore both the sinner and the Church to spiritual health.

But the main reason for going to confession is that we meet Jesus there. Christ has arranged to be present in the priest sacramentally, so that when we confess our sins, we are telling them to the Lord himself. What could be better than receiving forgiveness for our sins from the person who already loved us so much that he gave his life to free us from sin?

❧

Christianity gives a human face to the invisible grace of God. The Son of God became man so that in him we could more easily recognize God's merciful love for us. For the very same reason, his words of pardon are spoken to us in the human accents of his authorized representative.

Edward D. O'Connor, C.S.C.

For Discussion

• Why should we take sin more seriously? How does sin affect us? How does it affect the Church? Why did Jesus institute the sacrament of reconciliation? Why are we required to confess serious wrongdoing?

For Reflection

- When was the last time I went to the sacrament of reconciliation? What benefits would I experience from more frequent confession?
- Has everyone in my family made their first confession? What can we do to help all family members make more use of the sacrament?

Application Ideas

- Parents will not be able to interest children in the sacrament of reconciliation if they do not use it themselves. Our neglectful practice will have taught them that the sacrament is not important. So the first step to tapping the power of this sacrament is for parents to make confession a normal part of their own lives *before* they expect it of their kids. Here are some suggestions:
  - Mom and Dad should begin going to the sacrament once every four to six weeks.
  - They should have developed their reasons for regular confession so that they can explain to the children why it's important.
  - After the parents have established a pattern, they should involve the children in it.

Resources

Catechism of the Catholic Church, nos. 1440-1460; 1468-1470.
Peg Bowman, *At Home with the Sacraments: Reconciliation*
(Twenty-Third Publications: 1-800-321-0411).

40 Reconciliation Begins at Home

❦ *Family life is the school where we and our children learn the practice of reconciliation.*

"First be reconciled to your brother, and then come and offer your gift." Matthew 5:24

If we separate sacraments from life, we are not using them properly. The Lord intended them to be means of bringing the power of the Holy Spirit to bear in our ordinary lives. Sacraments are to be engaged in the realm of practice, not locked up in the realm of theory.

Because we live the Christian life in a community, reconciliation must move horizontally as well as vertically. For example, if we want to repair our relationship with God through the sacraments of reconciliation and the Eucharist, we must also be reconciled with sisters and brothers. We cannot have a good relationship with God when we are in a bad relationship with other people. So the Lord taught us that worshiping him required us first to set things right with someone we have offended.

Family life is the school where we and our children learn the practice of reconciliation. In our daily life together, we learn how to tap sacramental grace, engaging the help of the Spirit, to keep family relationships in good repair.

No matter how much love families have, they will always have conflicts. Personalities rub each other wrong at times. Preferences clash. We even deliberately hurt each other. So parents must be prepared to deal with broken relationships. To do this we must help the family apply the life-shaping principles Jesus gave us:

- "Love one another as I have loved you" (John 15:12).
- "Forgive, if you have anything against anyone" (Mark 11:25).

We can count on the Holy Spirit to help us apply these principles in our families.

Parents must develop mechanisms that instill love and forgiveness in the nitty-gritty of family life. For example, regularly telling kids that we love them is a practical tool for building solid family relationships. Equally important are down-to-earth ways to express forgiveness. When we offend another family member, we breach our relationship. We must take action to repair it. If we don't do something to close the gap quickly, things will rupture even more.

Parents should establish a formal way for the family to repair relationships. This involves creating an easy-to-use means for forgiving each other. In our home, for example, we bring aggrieved parties face-to-face. The "hurter" must say to the "hurtee," "I was wrong. Please forgive me." The "hurtee" must say to the "hurter," "I forgive you." That simple exchange restores the family relationship.

People in conflict don't feel like making up right away. "Hurters" are often willful and "hurtees" want revenge. But if we wait until we feel like repairing relationships, we'll wait a long time. We tell our kids that our family puts a priority on forgiveness. We explain that feelings are important but must take second place to family relationships. After they ask and give forgiveness, we help them with their hurts, anger, and guilt.

Parents must not excuse themselves from this practice. Moms and dads should ask forgiveness of children when they offend them and they should freely forgive their children, encouraging them to repent. You will find, as I have, that asking a child to forgive you for an outburst of anger wins respect. Dodging our wrongdoing spawns disrespect.

Seeking and granting forgiveness also helps husbands and wives keep their marital relationship healthy. When couples spat, they should resolve it right away without sleeping on it.

For Dad, Mom and all the children, reconciliation begins at home.

❦

You carry out the mission of the church at home in ordinary ways when you forgive and seek reconciliation. Over and over, you let go of old hurts and grudges to make peace with one another. And family members come to believe that, no matter what, they are still loved by you and by God.

U.S. Catholic Bishops

For Discussion

• What impact should our worship have on our relationships?
• Why should families have a means for seeking and granting forgiveness?

For Reflection

• What can I do to improve my relationships with other family members?
• How does worship at Mass affect my life? What can I do differently so that my worship will have a greater influence on my behavior?
• Does our family have a means in place for members to repair broken relationships?

Application Ideas

• Consider starting the practice of seeking and granting forgiveness as a way of repairing relationships in your family.

   Follow these guidelines:
   - Develop a clear picture of what you want to do and explain it to all the children.
   - Explain to the family that good relationships are expressions of Christian love and that the Holy Spirit will help you love and forgive each other.
   - Consider using role plays to teach the practice. Have one person be the "hurter" and another be the "hurtee."
   - Teach the hurter to say something like, "I was wrong to do X. Please forgive me." Teach the hurtee to say, "I forgive you."
   - Have family members resolve conflicts as quickly as possible on the day when they occur.
   - Instruct everyone that we respect their feelings, but we need to repair breaches before we feel like doing it. Seek and grant forgiveness now and your feelings will come along.

Resources

Catechism of the Catholic Church, nos. 1427-1439.
Charles and Margaret Savitskas, *How to Talk to Your Children About Reconciliation* (Our Sunday Visitor: 1-800-348-2440).

41 The Four Rs

 *The Lord wants sole-occupancy of our hearts, and it takes a lifetime for us to make the transfer complete.*

"Go, and do not sin again." John 8:11

We can easily get wrong ideas about our conversion to Christ. We can think that it's complete once we have made an adult Christian commitment. But it's not. Conversion is a lifelong process. The Lord wants sole-occupancy of our hearts, and it takes a lifetime for us to make the transfer complete.

We can also entertain the mistaken notion that conversion is mostly our work. For example, all the words that we use for steps in conversion suggest massive human effort — repenting, repairing relationships, doing penance, reforming. Performing these conversion activities makes it feel like we're doing all the work, and perhaps in a sense, it should, because we must be devoted to collaborating with God. But God is really the one causing our transformation.

The Lord initiates our transformation in baptism. He gives us the Holy Spirit as the source for our Christian growth. Then we must learn our part, the practical application of grace to our lives, which can be summed up under four Rs — Repentance, Reconciliation, Reparation, and Reform.

Repentance. Repentance is a dual turning — a turning from sin and a simultaneous turning to God. It involves honestly admitting our sin to God and to ourselves. Acknowledging what we have done wrong helps us take responsibility for it. Our sins get slippery if we make excuses for them, and we cannot pin them down to deal with them. But if we simply state, "I did that," we can do something about it. When we specify what we have done wrong, we can detest it and we can be sorry for having done it. Then we can decide to turn away from the sin and turn to the Lord.

Reconciliation. Sin damages our relationships with the Lord and with sisters and brothers. We repair our relationship with the Lord by confessing our sin to him. We can confess to him directly, but our main way of restoring our union with God is through the sacrament of reconciliation. If our sin has hurt others, we may need to be reconciled to them. We must tell them we are sorry for what we have done; then we may have to do something to make up for it. That comes under the next R.

Reparation. Reconciliation with God wipes away our sin, but it does not undo all the damage the sin may have caused. To repair the spiritual damage, the Church asks us to do penance. In the sacrament of reconciliation, the priest determines a penance as an appropriate reparation for our wrongdoing. If we did personal or material damage to another person, we must make up for it. For example, we may have to replace something we stole, repair something we broke in a rage, or restore a reputation we ruined by telling lies. But even apart from the sacrament, it's appropriate for us to do penance. Prayer, fasting, almsgiving, and service activities draw us nearer to the Lord and dispose us to obeying him. And obedience is essential to the fourth R.

Reform. We find reform the hardest conversion step because it requires us to change our behavior. We get comfortable with our sinful patterns and we may even like them. So it's difficult to trade them for new behaviors, but trade them we must. We must learn to replace fighting with peace, angry outbursts with patience, lying with truth-telling, hatred with love, and so on. These are the fruits of the Spirit that the Lord produces in us if we do what he tells us to do. Obedience is the expression of our love for the Lord, and loving the Lord is the goal of conversion.

❧

Do what you can and then pray that God will give you the power to do what you cannot.

St. Augustine

For Discussion

• What does "conversion to Christ" mean to you? Why is it important for us to honestly admit our wrongdoing? What role does the sacrament of reconciliation play in our conversion? Why must we do penance for our sins? What's involved in reforming our lives?

For Reflection

• Do I actively pursue my conversion to Christ? How well are family members informed about applying the graces of conversion to their lives? How can I begin to teach the children about the Four Rs in language they will understand?

Application Ideas

• Use the four Rs as a mirror for your Christian life. How well do you perform the actions associated with each of these conversion steps?

• Parents can teach children, even younger ones, the basic elements of the four Rs.

  - Repentance. When a child does something wrong, he or she can be taught to admit it honestly by being asked to say something like, "I knocked baby sister down. I'm sorry."

  - Reconciliation. Before children are old enough for confession, teach them to pray the act of contrition as a way of being reconciled to God. When they are old enough, suggest the sacrament.

  - Reparation. Teach children about doing penance during the Lenten season. For example, have them pray daily for strength in a special area of weakness or have them do something regularly to serve another family member or neighbor. When they do something wrong that causes damage, help them find a way to make up for it.

  - Reform. Help a child with a weakness or a fault by training him or her in behaviors that strengthen the child. For example, if a child is overly possessive, provide him with some small items that with your help he can learn to share with friends.

Resources

Catechism of the Catholic Church, nos. 1430-1439; 1459.
Benedict Groeschel, *Healing the Original Wound* (Servant Publications: 1-800-458-8505).

42 Preparing a Family for First Reconciliation

❦ *Parents' example is key to a family's getting in the habit of using the sacrament of reconciliation.*

Confess your sins to one another, and pray for one another, that you may be healed. James 5:16

My first confession was a disaster. I tried to read a laundry list of sins that Sister Electa had provided us second graders. Weary and impatient, Father Angel stopped me after sin number five — I think it was "presumption."

"That's enough!" he said, and I was out of there in no time.

Many parents have similar bad memories of their first confessions. Some don't remember much else about the sacrament of reconciliation because they have not used it. So when the time comes to prepare a child for it, we find ourselves blocked by fear, ignorance, or both.

We have to do something to get past these obstacles. Our example and leadership are key to our family's getting in the habit of using the sacrament of reconciliation. If we opt out, so will our kids.

Parents must get informed about the sacrament, especially about the new rites for celebrating it. We may remember dark confessionals, the priest behind a screen, lists of sins, occasional scoldings, absolution in Latin, penances at the altar rail. Things have changed. Anonymous private confession is still available, but more often reconciliation occurs face to face as the highlight of a communal penance service. The experience is less rigid, less legalistic, more conducive to receiving forgiveness and shedding guilt. Celebrating the sacrament in community shows that reconciliation is a corporate not a private matter and demonstrates the importance of our caring for each other's spiritual health. The experience is positive, not fearsome.

Here are some opportunities parents have to learn about the sacrament of reconciliation:

• Find out how your parish celebrates the sacrament. Ask your pastor or director of religious education to describe the available options and show you how to participate in them.

- Read a good introductory book about the sacrament of reconciliation.
- Take advantage of the parent classes in your parish's sacramental preparation program. If your parish does not have a program, get together with some other parents and request instruction.
- Plunge in by attending the next communal penance service at your parish. No better way to learn than by doing.

Preparing a child for first reconciliation can be an opportunity to trigger regular participation of the entire family in the sacrament. Even if that's just Mom and Dad, it's worth the effort. But it could be the chance to draw older children back to the sacrament and to prepare younger children for what's to come.

Consider these steps to involve the family:

- Find out if the parish encourages the family to join in the celebration of first reconciliation. If it does, have the child who is to celebrate first reconciliation invite all family members to participate in the event. If the parish does not involve families, plan to attend the next communal penance service together.
- Schedule mini-study sessions on the sacrament. Have the child share what he is learning, and use his books.
- Select a book on reconciliation and read it to the family.
- At family prayer times, read and discuss Scripture about God's mercy and forgiveness; for example, John 7:53-8:11 or Luke 15:11-32.
- Call attention to the penitential rite at the beginning of Mass, explaining that it is designed as a regular opportunity for us to repent of sin and to be reconciled with God.
- Talk about the family's practice of seeking and granting forgiveness. Repairing relationships among family members is a long-term preparation for seeking reconciliation with God in the sacrament.
- Ask family members to pray regularly for the child who will be making first reconciliation and to pray for each other. Praying

for each other's growth in Christ is a real expression of family love and support.

❧

An Act of Contrition

O God,
I am sorry with my whole heart for all my sins
because you are goodness itself
and sin is an offense against you.
Therefore, I firmly resolve,
with the help of your grace,
not to sin again and to avoid the occasions of sin.

For Discussion

• Why is it important for parents to participate regularly in the sacrament of reconciliation?

For Reflection

• What should we do to prepare our child for first reconciliation? How can we involve the whole family?

Application Ideas

• Review the suggestions made in the article. Decide which are most important to you and easiest to do in your family. Implement some of these choices.

Resources

Peg Bowman, *At Home with the Sacraments: Reconciliation* (Twenty-Third Publications: 1-800-321-0411).

Archbishop Daniel E. Pilarczyk, *The Catholic Guide to Confession* (Our Sunday Visitor: 1-800-348-0440).

Your Child's First Confession (Liguori Publications: 1-800-325-9521, ext. 657).

43  Healing the Sick

Through the sacrament of the anointing of the sick, Jesus continues to restore people to spiritual and physical health.

Is any among you sick? Let him call for the elders of the church, and let them pray over him, anointing him with oil in the name of the Lord; and the prayer of faith will save the sick man, and the Lord will raise him up; and if he has committed sins he will be forgiven. James 5:14-15

Jesus had a two-pronged ministry: he proclaimed the arrival of the reign of God and he healed people. He healed almost as much as he preached. Healing the sick was a sign of the greater healing Jesus would accomplish on the cross. By his death and resurrection, he performed a radical healing of humankind by overpowering the evil one. He destroyed sin and death, which are at the root of all our sicknesses, whether physical, psychological, or spiritual.

Jesus arranged for his healing ministry to continue in the Church by making it a sacrament. The Church sees the institution of the anointing of the sick in the training mission of the disciples. When Jesus sent the disciples out by twos, they healed many sick people by anointing them with oil (Mark 6:13). Christians anointed the sick from the earliest times, as we see in the letter of James, who wrote about the practice of the Jerusalem community sometime between A.D. 40 and 62.

For the first eight centuries, it was customary for priests and lay people to pray for healing, using oil blessed by the bishop to anoint the sick. As centuries passed, the sacrament evolved so that the priest alone anointed the sick, as part of preparing them for death. So the sacrament came to be regarded as "extreme unction" — the last anointing.

Since Vatican II, the Church has made this sacrament more accessible by offering it to the seriously ill and the aged infirm. Thus the Church restored the sacrament to its earlier role of strengthening and healing the sick physically and spiritually.

Now people can receive the sacrament when in danger of death from sickness or old age, and they can receive it as often as necessary. For example, a sick woman who recovers can be anointed again if she relapses, or an elderly man can be anointed again when his frailty becomes more pronounced. Because the Church no longer reserves the sacrament until just before death, we no longer call it extreme unction, but the anointing of the sick.

When Jesus healed, he touched people, using signs that produced the results they signified. For example, when he healed a man afflicted with deafness and a speech impediment, he put his fingers in the man's ears, spat, touched the man's tongue, looked up to heaven, sighed, and gave a command (Mark 7:33).

Touching also plays a key role in the sacrament. The priest lays hands on the sick or infirm person in silence. Then he prays for him or her. Then taking oil that has been blessed by the bishop, the priest anoints the forehead and hands of the sick person, saying, "Through this holy anointing may the Lord in his love and mercy help you with the grace of the Holy Spirit. May the Lord who frees you from sin save you and raise you up."

The anointing with oil causes what it signifies, a healing and strengthening of the soul, and sometimes a healing and strengthening of the body. So this sacrament may result in physical healing. But its main purpose is to strengthen a person spiritually so that he or she is prepared on death to enter heaven directly. As St. Thomas Aquinas said, by this sacrament "a person is prepared for immediate entry into glory."

Like all sacraments, the anointing of the sick is an action of the body of Christ. When this sacrament is celebrated privately, the sacrament of reconciliation customarily precedes it and the Eucharist follows immediately. Some parishes schedule communal celebrations of the sacrament during a Sunday liturgy, and invite the sick and infirm to receive, praying with the whole community present. Thus the body of Christ shows its care for sick and infirm members. When these suffering members are strengthened and healed spiritually and physically, the whole body, which suffers with them, is also restored to health.

☙

When we were baptized we were raised out of the purely natural sphere of life into community with God. We began to live divine life. . . . The anointing of the sick completes this process, throwing open the gate of heaven and preparing us for beatific vision. . . . The world of signs and symbols ceases and the reality of God, as he is, is our new sphere of life, of true and real life.

H. A. Reinhold

For Discussion

• What role did healing play in Jesus ministry? Why does the Church no longer call this sacrament "extreme unction"? What are the effects of this sacrament?

For Reflection

• How can I serve sick or aged relatives and friends? Can I arrange for them to receive the sacrament of the anointing of the sick? Have I prayed with them for their spiritual and physical health?

Application Ideas

• Find out when your parish or another local parish plans to have a communal celebration of the anointing of the sick. Have your family attend the service. Use the event as an occasion to talk about the sacrament.

Resources

Catechism of the Catholic Church, nos. 1511-1532.

Edward D. O'Connor, C.S.C., *The Catholic Vision* (Our Sunday Visitor: 1-800-348-2440), 406-407.

44 Healing at Home

🐛 *We should exercise our participation in Christ's ministry by praying for healing in our families.*

He . . . entered the house of Simon and Andrew, with James and John. Now Simon's mother-in-law lay sick with a fever, and immediately they told him of her. And he came and took her by the hand and lifted her up, and the fever left her; and she served them. Mark 1:29-31

Over the past thirty years our big family of seven children has had its share of sicknesses and accidents. They have ranged from minor cuts and colds, to broken bones, and hospitalizations for dehydration, one that nearly claimed the life of an infant son. One year when we had four children under seven, I think that we were on a first-name basis with the attendants at the local emergency room. If we hadn't shown up once a month, I imagine they would have called to ask where we had been. Always, my wife, Mary Lou, and I have taken a common-sense approach to these family illnesses and injuries, resorting to both natural and supernatural means of restoration.

When someone gets sick or hurt, we pray for the person. Our prayer includes laying on of hands because this gesture is a sign of love and faith. It disposes us and the sick person to receive the healing grace that comes from the Holy Spirit. We also use medicines, call the doctor, or rush to hospitals. Grace builds on nature, so we count on the Lord to work directly to make us well or, if he chooses, to use professionals to help us mend. Healing comes from the Lord's touch, whether he uses his own hands or the doctor's.

Jesus healed people because he loved them. He was himself the sign that the kingdom of God had come to earth, and his healings declared God's presence among us. The Lord's ministry of healing did not cease when he ascended to the Father. It had just begun. It continues among us in the body of Christ, which now makes known the presence of God on the earth.

Healing us on all levels — physical, psychological, and spiritual — is one of the Lord's main activities in the Church. That makes it one of our main concerns, too, because now in the body of Christ, his actions have become our actions. We share in his healing ministry through our participation in the sacraments:

- When we celebrate the sacrament of the anointing of the sick with an infirm or aged grandmother, we are praying for her physical and spiritual health.
- When we receive the sacrament of reconciliation, we obtain a spiritual healing that restores health to the whole body of Christ, which ails as long as sin afflicts even one member.
- When we participate in the Eucharist, we expect the Lord to touch and heal us. At communion, with the priest we pray: Lord, I am not worthy to receive you, but only say the word and I shall be *healed*.

The Church provides these sacraments for our healing, but also encourages us to pray for healing at home. By blessing someone with the sign of the cross and praying for him to get well, we are making use of a sacramental. A sacramental is an action that prepares us to receive grace and to cooperate with it. It is not a sacrament itself, but derives its spiritual energy from the sacraments. Our baptism, for example, gives us a share in Christ's priesthood, which we can exercise by blessing others.

Don't let inexperience or fear prevent you from praying for healing in your family. Gather everyone around the sick or injured person. Invite all to lay on hands gently. Make the sign of the cross over the person. In your own words, ask Jesus to heal the one who is ailing. Everyone at Simon Peter's house expected Jesus to heal his mother-in-law. Why shouldn't we expect the same Jesus, now dwelling in us in the body of Christ, to heal the sick people at our house?

❦

The healing of Jesus . . . is central to the doctrine of the gospel. To deny this is, in effect, to deny the gospel — to change it from the Good News to the Good Advice which lacks the power to transform humankind into a new creation. In short, Jesus did not heal people to prove that he was God; he healed them *because he was God*.

Francis MacNutt

For Discussion

• Why should we pray for healing in our families?
• In what sense do we share in Christ's healing ministry?

For Reflection

• On what occasions have I prayed for my own healing or for someone else's healing?
• Do we pray for healing in our family? What could we do in our family to benefit more from Christ's healing power?

Application Ideas

• Initiate the practice of praying together for sick or injured persons in your family. Prepare family members by talking about Jesus' healing ministry and our share in it through our participation in the body of Christ.
• To increase awareness of the Lord's desire to heal us, have a series of family Bible studies on Jesus' ministry of healing. Use the following passages. Either read them once a day for five days and discuss them, or assign them to different family members and invite each person to tell the story at a family prayer time. Be sure to discuss what the passages mean to the family.
    - Jesus cures a paralytic, Luke 5:17-26.
    - Jesus heals a centurion's slave, Luke 7:1-10.
    - Jesus heals the woman with hemorrhage, Luke 8:40-48.
    - Jesus heals the man born blind, John, 9:1-41.

Resources

Catechism of the Catholic Church, nos. 1499-1510.
Francis MacNutt, *Healing* (Ave Maria Press: 1-800-282-1865).
Michael Scanlan, *Healing Principles* (Servant Publications: 1-800-458-8505).

Empowered for Daily Living

66 *The whole mystery of the spiritual life
is that Jesus is forever being born in
us. The whole meaning of being a
Christian is to become bit by bit
transformed into Jesus Christ.* 99

Jean Danielou

45 Mary, Help of Christians

❦ *Devotion to Mary assists us in applying sacramental graces because she is an incomparable intercessor and model.*

When Jesus saw his mother and the disciple whom he loved standing near, he said to his mother, "Woman, behold, your son!" Then he said to the disciple, "Behold, your mother." John 19:26-27

The sacraments are the power and light utilities of the body of Christ. Baptism, for example, energizes our souls with the power of the Holy Spirit and the light of Christ. With divine power coursing through our lives, you might think that we would always obey God effortlessly. In fact, you might think that we would be so captivated by the Lord's presence, that we would never stray from doing the right thing.

With the gentlest revelation of his goodness, God could so intoxicate our spirits that we would never want to do anything except please him. But that's not how he works. The Lord has decided not to override our human liberty because he wants us to freely choose to give ourselves to him.

Consider Mary. Imagine how perplexed she must have felt when an angel appeared saying that God chose her to be the mother of his Son. (See Luke 1:26-38.) "How can this be?" she asked. "The Holy Spirit will accomplish it," said the angel. Not an entirely comforting answer to a virgin who would have to explain her pregnancy to the man she was to marry.

The Lord sent the angel to get Mary's consent because he respected her liberty and wanted her to choose. Even though the angel acknowledged that Mary was "full of grace," that grace left her free. She could have said no. But she freely decided to surrender her will and say yes to the Lord.

While our calling is not as extraordinary as Mary's, grace and freedom work in us the same way. The Lord floods us with grace, but waits for us to surrender to him freely. To tap the power of the sacraments, we must act — we must choose, say yes, say no, believe, pray, confess, love, and many other things. We need all the help we can get, and we could find no better helper than Mary, who cares for us with a mother's love.

The Lord gave Mary a significant role in his plan to redeem humankind, for she became the mother of the Savior. As the mother of Christ, she continues to serve in his body, the Church, by helping us come to her divine Son.

Mary prays for us and is a model of prayer for us. As an intercessor she has no equal. At Cana when the wine was running out, she merely hinted to Jesus that he might do something. His mother's request was enough to persuade the Lord to alter the timing of God's plan (John 2:1-11). Mary will intercede like that for us if we ask her.

But we can also follow her example and instruction. She told the servants at Cana to "do whatever he tells you," and they got to participate in a miraculous sign of God's presence. The more we do what he tells us, the more united we become to him, the more we can expect our prayers to be answered. That's what Jesus meant when he said we could ask anything in his name and the Father will do it for us (John 15:7, 16; 16:24). Like the servants at Cana, we may even get to participate in life-changing transformations.

As his mother, Mary had a special relationship to Jesus, but she was also his first disciple. This woman who brought Christ into the world is an exemplar for all of us who are now commissioned to bring Christ to our world. Among many things, Mary's example teaches us:

- Trust in God. Amid confusing circumstances, like those surrounding the annunciation, Mary was simply open to God and confident that he would work things out. We also face many perplexities and would do well to imitate her.
- Dedication to the Lord's plan of salvation. Mary's first concern was serving the Lord's work of redeeming humankind, a responsibility we share as baptized Christians.
- Perseverance. From Bethlehem to Calvary, Mary endured great sufferings. When we experience pain and sorrow, her example can inspire us and her prayers will help us.

Mary was present in the upper room at Pentecost and there

received the Holy Spirit with the other disciples. On that day she was united more closely to Jesus than she was when she carried him in her womb. She entered a personal relationship with the Lord in the Spirit that surpassed her human relationship with him. As Christians baptized in the Spirit, we have the same kind of personal relationship with Jesus. And Mary shows us how to conduct that relationship — how to love Jesus, serve him, praise him, obey him, and live our days with him in every way.

❧

The knot of Eve's disobedience was loosed by the obedience of Mary. What the virgin Eve had bound in unbelief, the virgin Mary loosed through faith.

St. Irenaeus of Lyon

For Discussion

• Why is it possible for us to act contrary to the influence of grace?
• In what ways does Mary help us tap the power of the sacraments?

For Reflection

• How has devotion to Mary helped me on my Christian journey?
• Do all family members understand Mary's role in God's plan?

Application Ideas

• The rosary is a collection of prayers that help us meditate on God's plan of salvation as it was fulfilled in the life of Christ.
  - Teach family members to pray the rosary.
  - Use the rosary at family prayers daily for a week.
  - Consider praying the family rosary once a week.
  - In the appendix, you will find the mysteries of the rosary with appropriate Scripture passages for each.

Resources

Catechism of the Catholic Church, nos. 2617-2622; 2673-2679.
Edward. D. O'Connor, C.S.C. *The Catholic Vision* (Our Sunday Visitor: 1-800-348-2440), 446-460.

46 <u>Songs God Loves to Hear</u>

> *When we pray the psalms, we join with Christ in the prayer he prays in his body, the Church.*

Sing to the LORD a new song, his praise in the assembly of the faithful! Psalm 149:1

From ancient times the Christian community has sanctified the day by praying with Christ at specified times. *The Liturgy of the Hours* is this official prayer of the Church. It hinges on morning prayer and evening prayer, and also includes other daytime and nighttime prayers. All consist mainly of psalms, but also contain biblical canticles and readings, responsories, and other prayers. The celebration of this formal prayer of the Church is an obligation for priests and members of religious orders, but all of us are encouraged to participate, even individually.

During my college years, I learned to love the psalms, and the psalms taught me to love the Lord. These wonderful Old Testament songs not only gave me the words that I could use to praise God, they brought me into God's presence and made me want to praise him. Thomas Merton said that the Church loves the psalms "because God has given himself to her in them, as in a sacrament." That sums up my lifelong experience in praying the psalms. When I recite their words and reflect on them, I sense my union with the Lord. I love the psalms because I meet Jesus in them.

Along with the Lord's Prayer, the psalms *are* the prayers of Christ. We know from Scripture that he prayed them as an individual human being, and now he prays them in the body of Christ. Vatican Council II said that when we pray the hours with the priest, as, for example, at a parish vespers service, "It is the very prayer which Christ together with his body addresses to the Father." We also enter into Christ's prayer when we pray *The Liturgy of the Hours* privately, and even when we pray individual psalms.

Like the Lord's Prayer, the psalms are the revealed word of God.

When we pray them, we are truly praying in the Spirit because we are using God's own words. By giving them to us, he has indicated that they are the songs he loves to hear. First sung by people who knew God intimately, the words of the psalms take us to their divine source. Their inspired praises increase our knowledge of God, and our new knowledge of God increases our desire to praise him. The psalms draw us closer to the Lord by communicating his mind and heart to us.

Because the psalms are so well fitted to human life and life in Christ, they are appropriate for family prayer. We have used them in our family as the heart of our prayer time for many years. Our children like to recite them responsorially — Mom and the girls pray one verse, and alternately Dad the boys pray the next and so on. I can't think of a better way to teach kids to pray than having them pray with Christ the songs that God loves to hear.

❧

God taught us to praise him, in the psalms, not in order that he may get something out of this praise, but that we may be made better by it. Praising God in the words of the psalms, we can come to know him better. Knowing him better we love him better, loving him better we find our happiness in him.

Thomas Merton

For Discussion
• Why can it be said that when we pray the psalms we are praying with Christ?

For Reflection
• On what occasions have I found praying the psalms beneficial? Should I consider using them more in my personal prayer?
• What benefits would my family get from praying psalms? How could we introduce psalms into our family prayer time?

Application Ideas
• When praying the psalms individually or in the family, start by acknowledging that you are praying with Christ. Traditionally the Church has used a verse from Psalm 51 for this purpose: O Lord open my lips and my mouth shall declare your praise.

- For the next week, pray one psalm each day during your personal prayer time. Use the same psalm, or select a different one for each day. You have 150 to choose from, but consider these suggestions:
    - Psalm 148 to join all creation in praising God.
    - Psalm 146 to express trust in God.
    - Psalm 138 to thank the Lord.
    - Psalm 130 to pray for mercy.
    - Psalm 131 to rest in God.
    - Psalm 1 to choose true happiness.
    - Psalm 6 to ask God's help in distress.
- Consider introducing psalms in family prayer time.
    - You will need Bibles or prayer books with psalms. Be sure to have enough copies so that everyone can participate easily. Two to a book encourages sharing.
    - Explain to the children what the psalms are and why the family should pray them.
    - Experiment with praying the verses alternately. It works best to have Mom in one group and Dad in the other.
    - In families with younger children who cannot read yet, the parents can read the psalm and have the children respond at the close with the doxology: "Glory to the Father, and to the Son and to the Holy Spirit, as it was in the beginning, is now and ever shall be, world without end. Amen."

Resources

Catechism of the Catholic Church, nos. 2586-2589.

Thomas Merton, *Bread in the Wilderness* (The Liturgical Press: 1-800-858-5450).

Thomas Merton, *Praying the Psalms* (The Liturgical Press: 1-800-858-5450).

47 Faith to Live By

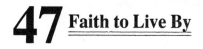 *Faith enables us to tap the power of the sacraments by believing God and trusting him to act in our lives.*

"He who hears my word and believes him who sent me, has eternal life." John 5:24

Human beings accept many things on faith. One of my older sons, for example, told me with some excitement that at Carlsbad Caverns he stood in an underground room big enough to hold a dozen Superdomes. I have not seen it myself, but I believe it on my son's word. Even when scientists change their minds, we believe their word: Last week margarine was healthy, this week it's not, so we're back to butter. Believing what we hear on the authority of someone else is a natural human thing to do.

But Christian faith surpasses the mere human act of taking someone at his word. It is an enhancement of our human nature that God accomplishes through the sacraments by allowing us to share his life. Faith is a supernatural empowerment that helps us live our eternal lives in down-to-earth ways. It comes in three varieties, each of which has practical implications for us — belief, trust, and expectation.

Belief. Human reason is powerful enough to tell us that God exists. We can recognize his reality in his creation from the vastness of the universe down to the infinitesimal world of atoms. But reason cannot tell us much about God and what he is like. For example, we have no natural way of figuring out that God is a Trinity. So in order that we might come to know him, God told us about himself and revealed some of his innermost thoughts in Scripture and in Jesus. He gives us the gift of faith so that we can grasp and believe in his truths. Thus faith is a grace that enhances our reason and expands our capacity to know God.

Trust. God does not just reveal truths for us to believe, but he reveals himself so that we can know him personally. So faith is not only an activity of the mind. It is also an activity of the heart. Faith opens our relationship with the Lord and enables us to continue growing closer to him. We call this heart dimension of faith "trust" because it causes us to rely on God.

We trust the Lord for the big things and for the little things. By God's grace we believe his plan of salvation that Jesus proclaimed, and our trust in him will bring us to our eternal happiness. It's also trust that gets us through our days. The Lord cares about the details of our lives. He shows his love for us by making our needs and hassles his own concerns. So the grace of faith affects our wills and prompts us to love God.

Expectation. The Lord reveals himself to us so that he can intervene in our lives and involve us in accomplishing his plan of salvation. He gives us the Holy Spirit who comes to empower us with gifts and graces. Faith opens us to the Lord's interventions, and expectation is the element in faith that engages the power of the Spirit.

For example, when the woman with a hemorrhage reached to touch Jesus' clothing, she was exercising this kind of faith. (See Mark 5:25-34.) Her faith engaged the Lord's power. Scripture says Jesus sensed that "power had gone forth from him," and he told the woman that her faith had made her well.

Similarly, expectant faith can help us experience the Lord's action. We can exercise it by asking the Lord to give us a fresh outpouring of the Holy Spirit and by expecting him to do it. Jesus said that if we know how to give good gifts to our children, "how much more will the heavenly Father give the Holy Spirit to those who ask him" (Luke 11:13).

The Holy Spirit empowers us and equips us for our work of continuing Christ's ministry through his body, the Church. So expectant faith activates the Holy Spirit in us, and he gives us the spiritual strength to serve the Lord and others.

Many of us learned in catechism class that God made us to know, love, and serve him in this life and to be happy with him in heaven. Faith in its three varieties helps us fulfill these purposes in practical ways: We believe so we can know God more fully, we trust him so that we can love him more, and we expect him to empower us so that we can serve him better.

The Apostles' Creed

I believe in God, the Father almighty, creator of heaven and earth; and in Jesus Christ, his only Son, our Lord; who was conceived by the Holy Spirit, born of the Virgin Mary, suffered under Pontius Pilate, was crucified, died, and was buried. He descended into hell, the third day he rose from the dead. He ascended into heaven, and is seated at the right hand of God the Father almighty. From there he shall come to judge the living and the dead.

I believe in the Holy Spirit, the holy Catholic Church, the communion of saints, the forgiveness of sins, the resurrection of the body, and life everlasting. Amen.

For Discussion

• In what practical ways does faith help us live the Christian life? How does it help us tap the power of the sacraments?

For Reflection

• In what ways has faith increased my knowledge of God? Do I trust God to help me with my problems? Do I ask the Lord to refresh me in his Spirit and expect him to do it?

• How can I help members of my family grow in faith?

Application Ideas

• Teach everyone in the family to pray the Apostles' Creed. Use it at family prayer every day for a month, and encourage all to use it regularly in personal prayer.

• Look for opportunities to speak with family members about your experience of the different kinds of faith, and ask them to talk about their faith experiences, too. We can occasion someone's growth in faith by telling them about our relationship to God.

Resources

Catechism of the Catholic Church, nos. 142-165.

Edward D. O'Connor, C.S.C., *The Catholic Vision* (Our Sunday Visitor: 1-800-348-2440), 104-113; 351-353.

48 Signs of Hope

 *Hope is the expectation of seeing God face to face, and it leads us to grow in holiness and love until we do.*

Let us hold fast the confession of our hope without wavering. Hebrews 10:23

When I was a Notre Dame graduate student, I worked for a wry professor who left students little room for hope.

"What if I read five extra books, then could I get an A?" a desperate student once asked him, the final petition in a litany of "what ifs." He was hoping to replace the F he had earned.

"What if you won the Nobel Prize for history?" replied the professor, toppling the young man's optimism.

Optimism gives a positive bent to our perspective until it bumps into an obstacle that knocks it down, as my professor's strictness did to the student's expectation. "Hope" of this sort fails us because ultimately it is groundless.

Hope, however, is altogether different from natural optimism because it firmly grounds its promise of future glory on the core reality of Christianity, the death and resurrection of Jesus. We do not acquire it naturally, like common sense, nor by habitual good behavior, like bravery. Hope is God's gift, a supernatural enhancement of our humanity that comes with our share in eternal life. It is the divinely-inspired, confident expectation that the Lord will keep his promises.

Through the sacraments of initiation, the Father has adopted us as his children. He has already given us many extraordinary blessings by taking our mere human lives up to the supernatural level. But there is much more that he still plans to give us. We are heirs, waiting for our full inheritance. The future glory that we await is our direct union with God. Scripture says that when the kingdom of God finally comes, we will see him as he is, face to face (1 Corinthians 13:12; 1 John 3:2).

Our hope is future-oriented, but it has significant practical implications for the present. We live now in a world that is twisted out of its true shape. We are subject to suffering of all sorts, and ultimately to death. So sometimes we groan in misery, even though we live in Christ. But Scripture says we have a companion who groans with us, the Holy Spirit who helps us in our weakness (Romans 8:23-26).

Hope is the spiritual equivalent of having read the last page of a mystery first — we already know how it is going to come out. Thus we can approach our lives with a certain anticipation, knowing that even in the face of discouragement or trials, the Lord will bring good out of evil.

Focusing on our hope of glory does not distract us from earthly concerns, but motivates us to pursue them with greater urgency. The New Testament, which was written at a time when many Christians expected the Lord to return at any moment, teaches that the imminence of the end should impel us to work even harder in the service of God's plan. The Lord has delayed the final coming of his kingdom, says St. Peter, so that we can repent ourselves and bring many more people to repentance (2 Peter 3:9). Thus hope leads us to love — to love the Lord more and to love others more by telling them that union with God is theirs for the asking.

The Church helps us by strengthening us in our hope and by constantly reminding us to see our ordinary lives in the perspective of eternity.

Every celebration of the Eucharist, in particular, is an anticipation of the heavenly banquet. Longing for the second coming is a theme that weaves through the prayers of the Mass, for example:

- "Christ has died, Christ is risen, Christ will come again!"
- "Protect us from all anxiety as we wait in joyful hope for the coming of our Savior, Jesus Christ."

Jesus himself connected the Last Supper with the final coming of God's kingdom (Luke 22:16, 18), and the liturgy brings this to mind at communion by inviting us to the supper of the Lamb.

The other sacraments are also signs of hope. They bring the glory of heaven to us on earth to prepare us for our heavenly glory.

Jesus is honey in the mouth, music in the ear, a shout of gladness in the heart.

St. Bernard of Clairvaux

For Discussion

• How does hope differ from optimism? How does hope help us in practical ways?

For Reflection

• Am I a hopeful Christian? How can I approach my life with more hope?

Application Ideas

• Individually or with family members, review the ordinary parts of the Mass from the opening prayer to the final blessing, looking for signs of hope. Notice prayers for everlasting life, the coming of the Lord, future glory, and so on.

Resources

Catechism of the Catholic Church, nos. 1817-1821; 2090.

Edward D. O'Connor, C.S.C., *The Catholic Vision* (Our Sunday Visitor: 1-800-348-2440), 348-351.

49 Schools of Love

 *The sacraments supernaturally magnify our capacity to love, and family life is the place we learn to apply it.*

"If I then, your Lord and Teacher, have washed your feet, you also ought to wash one another's feet." John 13:14

Have you ever known parents who were tempted to say with Bill Cosby's mother, "I brought you into this world and I can take you out of it?" I have felt that way. Sometimes children do things that are wrong, and parents may feel as though they deserve rejection. But we choose to love them anyway.

Commitment distinguishes Christian love from popular notions of romantic love, which tell us to love those we are attracted to. God made romantic love good, but we must not mistake it for Christian love. If we have confused these two loves, we may be mistakenly reserving our love for those who appeal to us and withholding it from those who don't. We may also be trying to stir up feelings of love, thinking that Jesus commanded us to feel attracted to others, but this is not the case.

As Christians, our love depends upon who we are, not upon who we love. We love because we are disciples of Jesus. His love for us and our love for him is the source of our love for others. If love depended upon who we loved, we would not love much. But we are free to love others regardless of who they are because love is the Lord's commandment, and we are committed to obey him. "A new commandment I give to you," Jesus said, "that you love one another; even as I have loved you, that you also love one another" (John 13:34).

Christian love is selflessly concerned for the interests of others. Romantic love focuses on the beloved, but it also has a strong selfish element. While love songs, for example, praise the one who is loved, they invariably proclaim, "I need you" or "I can't live without you." But there is nothing selfish about Christian love. It asks not "what can I get out of it?" but rather "what can I put into it?" Jesus, the archetype of love, had nothing to gain in his public ministry. He gave his all for us at great personal cost.

This kind of love is not humanly possible without the intervention of the Holy Spirit. The capacity to love as Jesus did is not natural to us. Baptism and the other sacraments of initiation add it supernaturally to our human nature. These sacraments magnify our human power to love, enhancing it so that we can love others with divine power. So putting love into action is a most practical way of releasing reservoirs of sacramental graces into our lives.

Love-in-action means serving and caring for others. It is measured more by our consistent self-giving than by depth of feeling. But this does not mean love is supposed to be cold or calculated, for it should be expressed warmly and affectionately.

I will never forget the way my mother's brothers and sisters responded to my father's early death. For at least a year, sisters and sisters-in-law seemed daily to be in and out of our house, talking to mother, bringing meals, and pitching in. One brother visited every Sunday night for several years to provide fatherly attention to us boys. Another brother employed mother when the family business had to fold. For many years all the uncles, aunts, and cousins gathered at our house on Christmas day, which was their way of filling up the emptiness my mother felt in that season. Their care was a school of love for me.

The Lord invites all of us to spend our lives loving others in ways that cost us. We lose our life bit by bit when we serve someone else with time we had reserved for ourselves. When we help a needy friend with money we were stashing to treat ourselves, we die a little. The little daily acts of love that chip away at our lives are not very dramatic nor newsworthy, but as they accumulate, they make us more like Christ.

❦

The Christian must remember that he is likely to be the only copy of the gospels that the non-Christian will ever see.

Philip Scharper

For Discussion

• What characteristics of Christian love distinguish it from romantic love?

- In what ways does putting love into action help us tap the power of the sacraments?

For Reflection

- How does my exercise of Christian love measure up against the standards of commitment, selflessness, and service? What can I do differently to love more like Jesus did?
- How can I teach family members about Christian love?

Application Ideas

- Jesus made love the peg on which everything else hangs. It sums up God's whole expectation for human beings. (See Mark 12:28-31.) Consider how you can make love the ruling principle in your family. Here are some suggestions you may find helpful:
    - Regularly at prayer times, have the family read and discuss Scripture on love.
    - Use the following passages one at a time either once a day during a week or once a week for seven weeks: Mark 12:28-31; John 13:1-15; John 13:34-35; John 15:12-17; 1 Corinthians 13:1-13; Romans 13:8-10; 1 John 4:19-21.
    - When discussing the passage, ask these questions: What was the writer trying to say? What is God saying to me now? What difference does it make? What can I do differently to apply it to my life?
    - Consider having all family members memorize the same key line from a passage. Take turns at prayer time reciting the verse and sharing what it means to you and how you can apply it.
- In all family relationships and situations, make love the test of conduct. Train family members to ask, "What is the loving thing to do now?" Because love is the standard Christ used to measure behavior, there's no more practical way to teach basic Christian morality to children, or adults for that matter.

Resources

Catechism of the Catholic Church, nos. 1822-1829; 1889; 20'1; 2069; 2196; 2658.

Edward D. O'Connor, C.S.C., *The Catholic Vision* (Our Sui day Visitor: 1-800-348-2440), 353-356.

50 The Most Daring Prayer of All

God gave us the Our Father so that we would be able to pray united with Christ, using his own words.

"Lord, teach us to pray, as John taught his disciples." Luke 11:1

"Our Father who art an Evan," prays the three-year-old, "Harold is thy name," and we all chuckle at his well-intentioned imitation. I think God smiles, too. I wonder how many of us have become so used to the words of the Lord's Prayer that, like that toddler, we say them without paying attention to what they mean. That's easy enough to do, because when we become familiar with anything, it tends to become routine.

The Our Father, however, is not just another prayer formula. It is the most extraordinary prayer of all. God himself gave us this prayer through his Son, Jesus, so that we would be able to pray with his own words.

The Lord's Prayer is central to Christian life and worship. It is at the core of Jesus' teaching (see Matthew 6:9-13), and the Church has always prayed it at significant moments during baptism, confirmation, and the Mass. Many early Christians prayed it at least three times a day, and many contemporary Christians still do.

The Our Father is the most daring prayer of all, for in it we mere humans dare to call God "Father." Our claiming God as Father would be outrageous had he not adopted us as daughters and sons, making us intimates in his divine family. The Father sent Jesus to redeem us so that he could beget us as his children, and he "sent the Spirit of his Son into our hearts, crying, 'Abba! Father!' " (See Galatians 4:5-6.) So the Lord's Prayer helps us tap the power of the sacraments because praying it activates our participation in the divine life we received at baptism.

Since this prayer has so much to do with our relationship to the Lord and with the way we live, we should not pray it casually or by rote. Rather we should pray the Our Father reflectively, meaning each word as we say it. You can use the following paragraphs to help you unpack its densely beautiful phrases and pray it from your heart.

Our Father who art in heaven. We come into God's presence to love him. We are not praying to a distant God, but to the Father's presence in our hearts that began at baptism. We call him "our" Father, not "my" Father, to acknowledge the relationship we have with sisters and brothers in the Church.

The first three petitions seek the Father's own desires:

Hallowed be thy name. The Lord revealed his name progressively as he unfolded his plan to restore all humanity to himself. This petition asks that God continue to manifest the holiness of his name, which means that we are earnestly desiring the fulfillment of his plan of salvation for humankind.

Thy kingdom come. Here we mainly pray for the final coming of the reign of God through Christ's return. We also ask for the establishment of his reign in our hearts, and we commit ourselves to work for justice and peace to extend his rule to all humanity.

Thy will be done on earth as it is in heaven. The Father has revealed his plan to restore all things in Christ by bringing everything in heaven and on earth under his lordship (Ephesians 1:9-10). We pray earnestly for the accomplishment on earth of this plan that has already been realized in heaven.

The last four petitions express confidence in God to supply the deepest needs of our hearts:

Give us this day our daily bread. We express our trust in the Father to provide all of our material and spiritual needs. The "us" indicates our solidarity with all human beings, and so our prayer for bread commits us to seek the establishment of justice for all. We are also seeking more than ordinary food. We are asking God to satisfy our hunger both for his Word in Scripture and for the Bread of Life in the Eucharist.

And forgive us our trespasses as we forgive those who trespass against us. We beg the Father to forgive our sins. But our hearts remained closed to his mercy unless we forgive everyone who has offended us, even our enemies.

And lead us not into temptation. We ask God to keep us from taking the road that leads to sin and to refrain from putting us to the test. If we are to persevere and obtain our final salvation, we must have the wisdom and strength to fight temptation and endure trials.

But deliver us from evil. As Jesus himself prayed for our protection from the evil one (John 17:15), we pray for the deliverance of the whole human family from his power. Christ has already won the victory that accomplishes the Father's plan of salvation for humankind. Now we petition for the grace to apply that victory.

These reflections just scratch the surface of this marvelous prayer that comes to us from the heart of the Trinity. We have a lifetime to plumb its depths.

Run through all the words of the holy prayers [in Scripture], and I do not think that you will find anything in them that is not contained and included in the Lord's Prayer.

St. Augustine

For Discussion

- Why is the Our Father central to Christian living? How does praying it help us tap the power of the sacraments?
- Discuss each of the seven petitions of the Our Father, explaining what you think it means.

For Reflection

- Do I pray the Lord's Prayer frequently? Do I pray it reflectively?

Application Ideas

- For the next week use the Our Father as an outline for personal prayer. Reflect on each petition and expand on it spontaneously.
- Be sure that all family members have memorized the Our Father. Explain to them the importance of the prayer and encourage them to pray it daily. Renew your efforts to have the family pray it together regularly.

Resources

Catechism of the Catholic Church, nos. 2777-2856.
Edward D. O'Connor, C.S.C., *The Catholic Vision* (Our Sunday Visitor: 1-800-348-2440), 104 -113; 351-353.

Further Information

You will find many resources by referring to the catalogs of Catholic publishers. You can request them by phone:
- Abbey Press (812-357-6611)
- Ave Maria Press (1-800-282-1865)
- Franciscan University Press (614-283-3771)
- Ignatius Press (1-800-537-0390)
- Liguori Publications (1-800-325-9521, ext. 657)
- The Liturgical Press (1-800-858-5450)
- Our Sunday Visitor (1-800-348-2440)
- Paulist National Catholic Evangelization Association (1-800-237-5515)
- Servant Publications (1-800-458-8505)
- St. Anthony Messenger Press (1-800-488-0488)
- St. Paul Books & Media (1-800-876-4463)
- Twenty-Third Publications (1-800-321-0411)
- United States Catholic Conference (USCC) Office of Publishing Services (202-541-3090)

Pattern for Catholic Parent Meetings

Catholic parents can obtain essential support for their work of raising kids in the faith by participating in small communities. These groups should meet weekly or biweekly for prayer, study, growth, mutual encouragement, and accountability.

Participants can choose to study books like *50 Ways to Tap the Power of the Sacraments* that are designed for group use. Leadership should rotate among the couples, and all should make a commitment to attend regularly and to participate actively.

Sample Meeting Agenda*
- Prayer and Scripture (10 minutes)
- Discussion (25 minutes)
- Family-Life Review (25 minutes)
- Closing prayer (5 minutes)
- Social time (25 minutes)

*The times on the agenda are recommended so that meetings can be limited to 1-½ hours, but can be adjusted to meet local needs.

Family-Life Review
- Each parent or couple shares briefly on each question:
- What is the Lord teaching me about raising my children Catholic?
- What successes have I had in caring for my family in the past two weeks?
- What main needs do I see in my family now?
- What was my action plan for the past two weeks? Was it successful? What is my action plan for the next two weeks?

Sample Closing Prayer
- Each couple/parent states a need.
- Individuals pray spontaneously each for one need.
- Close with the Lord's Prayer.

Meeting Through the Year

- Long-term groups work best.
- Consider beginning with three units of three months each. For example, September through November; December, no meeting, family Christmas party; January through March; April through June; summer off. Schedule occasional family events.

Raising Kids Catholic Workshops

Presented by Bert Ghezzi

The _Keeping Your Kids Catholic_ workshop teaches parents an easy to use five-step approach to introducing Catholic truths and practices in the home.

Tapping the Power of the Sacraments is a workshop that teaches parents practical ways to help every family member apply sacramental graces to their lives.

Help and Hope for Catholic Families is a workshop for diocesan and parish leaders, teachers, and interested parents that focuses on how to equip parents to confidently assume their role in handing on the faith to their children.

Each workshop provides a vision and practical approaches for raising Catholic families. Participants are led to select and to plan the implementation of actions that are both important and easy to accomplish.

Participants enjoy talks, small-group discussions, personal reflections, questions and answers, role plays, activities, action plans, worship, and fellowship.

For more information write to:

Raising Kids Catholic Workshops
P.O. Box 1902
Winter Park, FL 32790

Special Offer: Free Audiocassette
"Show and Tell — How to Lead Children to Christ and the Church"
by Bert Ghezzi

To receive this free one-half hour tape, send your name, address, including zip code, to Special Offer, _Raising Kids Catholic_ at the above address.